THREE WAGNE

THREE WAGNER ESSAYS

translated by
Robert L. Jacobs

EULENBURG BOOKS
LONDON

Ernst Eulenburg Ltd
48 Great Marlborough Street
London W1V 1DB

Copyright © 1979 Ernst Eulenburg Ltd

This edition first published 1979
by Ernst Eulenburg Ltd

ISBN 0 903873 55 9 (cased)
      0 903873 56 7 (paperback)

Printed and bound in England by
Caligraving Ltd, Thetford, Norfolk

Condition of sale: This book is sold subject to the condition that it shall not, by way of trade or otherwise, be lent, re-sold, hired out or otherwise circulated without the Publisher's prior consent, in any form of binding or cover other than that in which it is published and without a similar condition including this condition being imposed on the subsequent purchaser.

CONTENTS

Translator's acknowledgments — vii
Translator's introduction — viii
I. 'Music of the Future' — 11
II. On Conducting — 45
   Translator's note — 47
   Motto from Goethe — 48
III. On Performing Beethoven's Ninth Symphony — 95

TRANSLATOR'S ACKNOWLEDGMENTS

For my rendering of '*Music of the Future*' I owe a great debt to Geoffrey Skelton. The work he put into it amounted to a collaboration, and was indeed intended as such (having collaborated in a re-translation of Wagner's early writings, published under the title, *Wagner Writes from Paris*, our plan, which circumstances prevented us from carrying out, was to produce a re-translation of some of his later ones).

For my rendering of *On Conducting* I took advantage of W. Ashton Ellis's ill-written but consistently faithful translation of Wagner's collected prose works and of the re-translation that Edward Dannreuther made of the essay, which is freer and more readable, albeit in places too free. Together they both helped me over one or two difficult hurdles.

TRANSLATOR'S INTRODUCTION

These three prose works of Wagner have been selected for re-translation because '*Music of the Future*' is the only succinct, attractively written and comparatively balanced account he gave of his art and aesthetic standpoint, and *On Conducting* and *On Performing Beethoven's Ninth Symphony* the only ones in which, without avoiding technicalities, he concentrated upon purely musical topics. Other pieces from the six volumes of his translated prose works might have been chosen: the blanket-term 'prose work' conceals their variety, their manifold degrees of worth and worthlessness. This book skims the cream to the extent that it presents Wagner at his most persuasive on the subject of his own art and on the other hand the principles and methods of the first great subjective conductor (embodied in our age by Fürtwangler) which have left a permanent imprint upon the world of public music-making.

That '*Music of the Future*' is succinct, attractively written and comparatively balanced is largely due to the circumstances of its composition. It was written in 1860. After his long sojourn in Switzerland, where he had written megalomaniacal theoretical treatises, two-thirds of the *Ring* and *Tristan*, Wagner settled in Paris in the autumn of 1859 in order to bring about a production of *Tannhäuser* and create interest in *Tristan*. A French friend had suggested that something should be done to dispel the impression, created by critics exasperated by *The Art-work of the Future* and *Opera and Drama*, that Wagner was a phantasist endeavouring to foist upon the world a crazy 'Music of the Future' (Zukunftsmusik'); Wagner accordingly arranged for a prose translation of the poems of *The Flying Dutchman*, *Tannhäuser*, *Lohengrin* and *Tristan*, together with the translation of an explanatory foreword, cast in the form of an open letter to the French friend, Frédéric Villot, who had made the suggestion. Villot, a curator at the Louvre, had been initiated into Wagner's works by Saint-Saëns, a fabulous sight-reader; in *Mein Leben* Wagner says he had a feeling of 'genuine attachment' ('ernstliche Zuneigung') to Villot and this feeling manifests itself in the open letter. Its German publication shortly after as a brochure, to which Wagner gave the title '*Zukunftsmusik*'– adopting his detractor's catchword: hence the inverted commas – was sub-titled *Brief an einen französischen Freund*. As a correspondent Wagner always tuned his style to his mental image of the addressee. Here he was addressing a friend who he knew loved and understood his music.

'*Music of the Future*', I said, gives a comparatively balanced account of Wagner's art and aesthetic standpoint. In Switzerland he had proclaimed that a neo-Hellenic Total Art-work (*Gesamtkunstwerk*) was the *summum bonum* of art. Painting was static; literature could not convey pure feeling; music could do just this, but was incapable of defining the feeling. Music could therefore be compared to a woman needing to be impregnated by dramatic poetry. This is now toned down. Music is acknowledged to be self-sufficient. But the acknowledgment is qualified: music's indefinite expression raises a 'disturbing question: "Why?"'; and it is the dramatic poet's function to provide an 'answer which would, as it were by circumvention, prevent it . . . from ever being put'. However, a subsequent paragraph undermines that qualification by observing that the classical composer 'maintains a certain reserve' preventing him from reaching a pitch of 'tragic passion' that would raise disturbing questions. And the tone of the essay as a whole makes clear that Wagner did not think any less of Beethoven's symphonies for that. Indeed it is with Beethoven in mind that he defines in memorable words the quintessence of his art: 'channelling into the bed of music drama the great stream that Beethoven sent pouring into German music'.

On Conducting was written in 1869, nine years later. During those years many Germans saw that 'great stream' pouring powerfully on in the instrumental and choral music of Brahms. Furthermore the performance earlier that year of the *Rhinegold* in Munich brought about by Ludwig under a conductor not of Wagner's choice opened the appalling prospect of the *Ring* being presented to the world piecemeal in performances not under his control. Perhaps, then, it is not surprising that *On Conducting*, which was written a month after that performance of the *Rhinegold*, is disrupted by passages neither succinct, attractive nor balanced – indeed so seriously disrupted that I have presented this translation in an abridged form. The early part of the essay is an agreeably caustic, historically valuable survey of contemporary concert-giving. Wagner then gives his prescriptions for conducting symphonies and overtures by Beethoven, Mozart and Weber. An amusing example of the mishandling of Tannhäuser's Narration brings him to the field of opera. But instead of entering it he returns to instrumental music in order to vent his spleen against the neo-classical establishment in a sneering, anti-semitic diatribe of over six-thousand words. This I have cut. Re-entering the field of opera, after a few general observations he proceeds to the climax of the essay: his prescriptions for conducting the overture to the *Mastersingers* and the opera itself. And then on the heels of this climax comes the anti-climax of *another* similarly unpleasant diatribe of over fifteen-hundred words! This too I have cut.

I have also taken another liberty.

Wagner once declared that it was pointless to write about musical technicalities since the reader would either not understand or else know what you meant already. Perhaps this has to do with why in *On Conducting*, which was originally published serially in *Die Neue Zeitschrift für Musik* and *New-Yorker Musik-Zeitung*, the music examples are so skimpy: the reader would be assumed to be so familiar with the music referred to that he would need no more than an occasional brief quote as an *aide mémoire*. I have amplified some of these brief quotes and added some more substantial ones.

On Performing Beethoven's Ninth Symphony was written in 1873. Its purpose was to recommend certain alternatives to the scoring, expression-marks and even to the notes, which had occurred to Wagner when he conducted the symphony the previous year in the rococo opera house at Bayreuth, on the momentous occasion of the laying of the foundation-stone of the *Festspielhaus*. No less a person than Felix Weingartner adopted nearly all Wagner's recommendations, with one or two amendments.[1] The same can be said of most conductors today – though of course they vary in the recommendations they adopt and the amendments they make. Ernest Newman's statement apropos of this essay that Wagner's proposals remain the 'starting point for all discussion of the technical problems that confront us in the master's last works'[2] still holds good.

The essay was published serially in the *Musikalisches Wochenblatt*. It suffers even more acutely than *On Conducting* from deficient musical illustration: Wagner was obliged to justify his proposals in detail and this he does so thoroughly that the essay is unintelligible to a reader who does not have the full score either in his head or at his elbow. With my publisher's permission I have supplemented his brief quotations with relevant extracts from the full score.

Robert L. Jacobs

---

[1] See Weingartner's essay on the Ninth Symphony in *Three Essays by Weingartner* (New York), 1969.
[2] *Life of Richard Wagner*, Vol. IV, p. 388

I
'Music of the Future'

'MUSIC OF THE FUTURE'

Honoured Sir,

You have invited me to give an account of certain ideas of mine published several years ago in a number of writings in Germany, where they attracted sufficient attention, not to say hostility, to make me an object of interest and curiosity in France. In view of the forthcoming performance of a music-dramatic work of mine in Paris you emphasized the importance of my doing this; you were so friendly as to assure me that a considered exposition of my standpoint would dispel errors and preconceptions and so make it easier for a prejudiced critic to confine his judgment to the work itself, without feeling obliged at the same time to concern himself with theories of a questionable nature.

It would, I confess, have been extremely hard to respond to that kindly meant invitation if you yourself had not pointed the way by offering to publish at the same time a translation of my opera texts. It would have seemed utterly impossible to immerse myself once more in that labyrinth of abstract speculation; indeed the revulsion I now feel at the thought of re-reading my theoretical works makes me realise what a thoroughly abnormal state of mind I was in when I wrote them, a state of mind which may occur once in the life of an artist but can hardly be repeated. Permit me first of all to describe that state as I regard it now; proceeding from the depiction of a subjective mood I shall then be able to present the concrete substance of theories whose recapitulation in a purely abstract form is now beyond me and would in any case hinder the purpose of this communication.

If we view the whole of Nature as broadly speaking a development from unconsciousness to consciousness and Man as the most striking example of the process, then undoubtedly the life of the artist is one of its most interesting manifestations, seeing that it is through artists and their creations that the world reveals itself and achieves conscious form. Not that this urge of the artist to represent is not itself inherently unconscious and instinctive. Even when he is forced to take thought – as he is when engaged in the task of applying his technical skill to the objective shaping of his intuitions – it is not really in the light of reflection that the artist reaches his decisions, but rather through an instinctive impulse which characterizes the nature of his gift. Sustained reflection is only demanded when he encounters some great obstacle in the employment of his expressive means, that is to say, when his ability to make his artistic purpose clear is constantly being hindered or even prevented entirely. The more dependent he is, not only on inanimate objects, but on the active co-operation of other artists, the greater the obstacles. A dramatist needs this co-operation in the fullest sense of the word if his work is to be effectively rendered; he must look to the theatre which, as the embodiment of representational art, follows its own peculiar laws. Stepping into this realm, he is entering what is already an artistic sphere in its own right, and if his intentions are to be realized he must let himself be absorbed into its peculiar being. If his tendency is in accord with that of the theatre there is no danger of misunderstanding: all that has to be considered is the character and degree of the accord. If his tendency is a completely different one, then of course it is another matter. The dilemma of the artist who is dependent upon an institution, framed to serve a purpose other than his own, needs no emphasis.

It was because I found myself in this dilemma that I felt compelled at a certain period of my life to bring to a halt my career of more or less unconscious artistic creation in order to arrive at an understanding of my problem by making a thorough investigation of its causes. I felt I could justifiably assume that no artist before me had ever been so sorely beset, since the artistic elements involved had never clashed so variously and so uniquely as here, where music and poetry on the one hand and modern forms of stage presentation on the other had to join forces with that most dubious and ambiguous of public institutions, the opera house of today.

Let me start by pointing to what I consider to be a crucially important distinction between the attitude of French and Italian composers and that of German ones to opera. This is so significant that you will easily understand why the problem in question could have arisen in the mind of a German composer and no other.

In Italy, where opera first developed, the composer's sole function was to write a number of arias for certain specified singers, whose dramatic talent was a subordinate consideration: the object was to provide vocal virtuosos with an opportunity to display their powers. Libretto and scenery merely provided the requisite dimensions of time and space. Singers alternated with dancers, and what they danced to was just the same as what was sung: all the composer had to do was to supply variations to a set type of aria. Agreement was possible down to the tiniest detail, since the composer was writing for specific singers whose individuality determined the precise character of the variations to be supplied. Italian opera thus became a *genre* in itself, having no connection with real drama, or even for that matter with true music: the connoisseur dates the decline

'Music of the Future'

of Italian music from the rise of Italian opera, a judgment illuminating to anyone who has experienced the nobility, the richness, the ineffable expressive depth of the Italian choral music of previous centuries, and who after a performance of, for example, Palestrina's *Stabat Mater* must find it impossible to regard Italian opera as the legitimate offspring of that wonderful mother.... But I mention this only in passing: for the present all that needs to be borne in mind is that in Italy up to this very day perfect harmony reigns between the institution of opera and those who compose for it.

The same could be said of opera in France, except that there singers and composers have a more difficult task, because the role of the librettist is so much more important. The national character and a significant development in dramatic poetry and dramatic art in the immediately preceding period inevitably meant the application of theatrical standards to opera. In 'grand opera' a definite style was evolved, founded on the rules of the *Théâtre français* and containing all the conventions and requirements of a dramatic performance. I shall not attempt to describe it; suffice to say that here you had a model theatre imposing its style on performer and author alike; that the author had before him a precise framework to be filled with action and music, and that he could rely on specific well-schooled singers and actors with whom he could work in complete agreement.

Opera came to Germany as a finished foreign product utterly alien in spirit to the German character. It began when German princes started summoning to their courts Italian opera companies together with their composers – German composers were obliged to go to Italy in order to learn how to write operas. Later on you had the theatres presenting French operas in translation. Such German theatres as there were amounted to no more than imitations of the foreign model sung in the vernacular. There was never any central theatre which could be regarded as a model. What with the Italian style, the French style and the German imitations of both all jumbled together, anarchy was complete. There were indeed attempts to build up the primitive and undeveloped *Singspiel* into a popular independent *genre*, but these were usually defeated by the foreigners' superior skill.

It goes without saying that under these conditions performances totally lacked style. In the smaller towns with only a limited public of regular opera-goers the repertoire could only be managed by ringing the changes on Italian operas, French ones, German imitations of either and German operas based on the lowliest kind of *Singspiel*. Some of these works were serious, others comic, but all were performed by one and the same cast. Roles designed for the finest Italian virtuosos were ridiculously travestied in a language utterly alien in character to the original by singers with no training and no vocal flexibility. And then you had the French operas, depending for their effect on a stylized declamation of sharply pointed phrases presented in hair-raising unmetrical translations hastily concocted for a miserable fee by translators who usually completely ignored the connection between the declamatory words and the music. This state of affairs was enough to prevent the development of a proper expressive style, since it led to singers and public not bothering about the text at all. Thus wherever you looked you saw incompetence: no well-run opera house setting the tone; available voices either inadequate or else totally untrained; everywhere utter artistic anarchy.

You will now understand that, from the point of view of a serious composer, there *was* no opera in Germany. If his inclinations or training pointed that way he had to write in Italian for the Italian opera or in French for the French opera. While Mozart and Gluck were engaged in writing Italian and French operas, a truly national music was evolving in Germany, but one which had nothing to do with opera. Ignoring that entirely and starting out from the branch of music upon which the Italians turned their backs when they created opera, German composers from Bach to Beethoven brought true music to that summit of glory which has earned German music universal recognition.

When a German composer looked beyond his great heritage of instrumental and choral music to dramatic music, he could find in the existing *genre* of opera no form to arouse his respect and, in its relative refinement, to serve as a model. The oratorio and especially the symphony provided noble, perfect models: opera offered nothing but a mish-mash of petty undeveloped forms cramped by meaningless conventions. To understand what I mean you have only to compare the magnificently developed form of Beethoven's symphonies with the musical numbers of his opera *Fidelio*. At once you sense how confined and frustrated the master felt, how he was hardly ever able to let loose his full powers – which was why, in order just once to let himself go completely, he flung himself with such desperate energy on the overture and cast it into a piece of unprecedented weight and significance. After this solitary attempt at an opera he gave up, discouraged – and yet he never relinquished the hope of finding a libretto through which his musical genius might be fulfilled. The *ideal* was always in his mind.

And indeed what was more natural than that the German composer confronted by the *reality* of the unsatisfying, problematic *genre* of opera, by which he was alternately attracted and repelled, should begin to think of it in *ideal* terms? Here we have the tendency which has given German artistic endeavour its distinctive stamp, not only in music, but in practically every other sphere. In what follows allow me to dwell on this a little more closely.

It cannot be denied that at an early stage the Latin nations of Europe had one great advantage over the Teutonic ones – namely, their superior cultivation of form. While Italy, Spain and France, in life as well as in art, developed pleasing, appropriate forms that soon became generally recognized and systematically applied, Germany was sunk in a state of anarchy, which its attempts to employ the forms of other nations did not conceal, but on the contrary aggravated. Among the obvious disadvantages – and how many there were! – was the slow development of German art and literature; not until the latter part of the eighteenth century did any movement arise comparable to what the Latin nations had achieved in the Renaissance. The German movement could in the nature of the case at first only have been a reaction against the distorted and distorting foreign form. Since there was nothing truly German which, having been once suppressed, could now be restored to its proper place, the movement then devoted its energies to discovering an ideal, purely human art transcending the barriers of nationality. The distinctive significance of Goethe and Schiller, Germany's two greatest poets, was that, as never before in the history of art, they concerned themselves with the problem of an ideal, purely human art in its most comprehensive sense – indeed one might almost say that the quest for such an ideal art was also the main ingredient of their works. Although they chafed against the tyranny of the form which among the Latin nations had the authority of law, they evaluated it objectively, taking cognizance both of its virtues and its defects; from this standpoint they then looked back to the art of ancient Greece, the cradle of all European art forms, and arrived at a full comprehension of the antique form. This led to the conception of an ideal, purely human art, liberated from narrow national conventions and yet at the same time capable of developing and transforming those very conventions into purely human, eternally valid laws.

The disadvantage under which the Germans had suffered was thus converted into an advantage. A Frenchman subjects himself to the apparently unalterable laws of a satisfying form congruent in every part; he commits himself to a perpetual reproduction, and hence to a certain stagnation (in a higher sense). On the other hand the German, though he sees the Frenchman's advantage, perceives also his handicap, the lack of freedom; thus he is able to envisage an ideal in which the validity inherent in every art form would be presented, stripped of everything accidental and untrue; unhampered by the barriers of nationality; *universally* accessible, and hence immeasurably significant. If differences of language prevent literature from attaining universality, music – that great language all men understand – should have the power, by dissolving verbal concepts into feeling, to communicate the innermost secrets of the artist's vision – especially when it is raised through the medium of a dramatic performance to that clarity of expression hitherto reserved to painting alone.

Here, rapidly outlined, you have the basis of that artistic ideal which became ever clearer to me and which I once felt compelled to describe fully in theoretical terms. This happened at a time when a mounting aversion to the *genre* of opera, which in my eyes bore to that ideal the frightening resemblance of an ape to a human being, took such possession of me that I had to flee far away into complete retirement.

To enable you to comprehend that period in my life, allow me, without boring you with biographical details, to depict the peculiar dilemma of a contemporary German composer who, with the symphonies of Beethoven engraved upon his heart, felt the need to come to terms with opera in Germany as I have described it.

Although I had a solid academic education, I was from the earliest period of my youth in close contact with the theatre. That period coincided with the last years of Carl Maria von Weber, who from time to time performed his operas in Dresden, where I lived. I received my first musical impressions from this master, whose melodies filled me with deep emotion and whose personality fascinated me. His death in a far country filled my young heart with horror. I first heard about Beethoven when I was told too of his death, which occurred not long after; then I got to know *his* music, likewise drawn to it by the mysterious news of his death. My bent for music, stimulated by these sombre impressions, grew ever stronger. Nevertheless it was only later, after other studies had led me into the field of classical antiquity and had inspired attempts at writing poetry, that I began to apply myself to music really thoroughly. I decided to write some music for a tragedy I had written. Rossini is said to have asked his teacher whether an opera composer needs to learn counterpoint. With Italian opera in mind, the teacher replied in the negative, and so the pupil gladly let it alone. *My* teacher initiated me into all the most difficult skills of counterpoint and, after he had done so, told me: 'Probably you will never have occasion to write a fugue. All the same, the fact that you *can* write one will give you technical confidence and make everything else easy.' Thus schooled, I took up the career of a theatrical music director and started composing operas to texts written by myself.

These few biographical particulars will suffice: after what I have said about the state of opera in Germany you will now easily be able to picture how my career developed. The peculiar gnawing pain I felt when I was conducting our routine operas often gave way to moments of inexpressible enthusiasm and well-being. This happened during the staging of works of a nobler kind when, in the heat of performance, the incomparable effect of drama combined with music was borne in upon me – an effect of depth and inwardness and yet of immediacy and vividness such as no other art is capable of. It was because I kept on experiencing such moments – revealing like lightning flashes undreamt-of possibilities – that I remained chained to the theatre, revolted though I was by the stereotyped nature of our opera productions. Among impressions of particular vividness I recall the performance in Berlin of a Spontini opera under the composer's own baton; I remember too how uplifted and ennobled I felt rehearsing Méhul's lovely *Joseph* with a small opera company. And during my lengthy sojourn in Paris, some twenty years ago, the productions of the Grand Opéra, with their expert musical and dramatic *mise-en-scène*, could not fail to dazzle and incite me. By far the most striking impression of all, though, was made in my early youth by a dramatic singer of – to my mind – unsurpassed stature: Wilhelmine Schröder-Devrient. Paris – perhaps you yourself – had the opportunity of hearing this great artist in her prime. The incomparable talent of this woman, the inimitable harmony and individuality of her interpretations, which I myself was actually witnessing with my own eyes and ears, held for me a magic which was to determine the whole direction of my career. I realised what such efforts could achieve and, with them in mind, there arose in me a consistent image, not only of what a singing and acting performance should be, but also of the poetic and musical shape of a work of art which I could hardly call by the name of opera. It grieved me to see this artist, driven by the need to find material for her talent, playing in pieces of the most insignificant kind and, while I was astounded by the depth and thrilling beauty of her Romeo in Bellini's feeble opera, this did not prevent my saying to myself: 'What an incomparable work of art that would be which was in every respect worthy of the histrionic talent of such an artist or a company of such artists!'

The higher the conception which, thanks to all this, I built of what opera could achieve, and the more clearly I came to envisage how the conception might be realized – namely, by channelling into the bed of music drama the great stream which Beethoven sent pouring into German music – the more depressed and disgusted I became with my daily intercourse with the actual operatic world, so infinitely removed from my ideal. Spare me a description of the intolerable chagrin of an artist becoming ever more aware of the possibility of creating a work of incomparable perfection, yet bound to a treadmill of daily activity in an institution whose conduct is the exact opposite of the ideal that possesses him. All my attempts at reform, all my proposals aimed at getting the institution [the Dresden Opera] to adopt a policy which would promote the ideal I strove for – as it could have done merely by adopting as the standard for all its achievements the excellence it did sometimes attain, however rarely – all these efforts fell through. All too clearly I learned what the modern theatre, and opera in particular, amounted to; so in disgust and despair I abandoned all hope of reform and ceased to bother myself with that frivolous institution.

I had now been supplied, in the most compelling and personal way, with a motive for trying to find an explanation for the incorrigible state of the modern theatre in the social function that it serves. Undeniably it was a mad idea on my part to try to make an institution committed almost exclusively to the business of diverting and entertaining a bored, pleasure-loving public and dependent upon earning enough to pay its way – undeniably it was mad of me to try to make such an institution serve the precisely opposite function of tearing the public away from its daily concerns in order to behold the highest and deepest of which the human mind is capable. I now had time to consider why the theatre served the function it did and to envisage the kind of society that would presuppose the theatre of my imagination as present-day society presupposes the present one. As I found a basis for my dramatic ideals in the individual achievements of a few great artists, so history provided me with a precedent for my conception of the ideal function a theatre should serve. I found that precedent in the theatre of ancient Athens, whose doors were open only on days of sacred festivals; where the enjoyment of art was at the same time a religious ceremony; where eminent citizens participated as poets and performers, appearing like priests before the assembled town and country folk – an audience keyed up to the highest expectations, before whom Aeschylus and Sophocles could present the profoundest poems ever written, knowing they would be understood.

Sadly I asked myself why so incomparable an artistic activity should have declined. It did not seem hard to explain. I considered in the first place the social reasons and assumed that these were bound up with the causes of the decline of the ancient city-state itself. I then attempted to frame the fundamentals of a social order that would make good the failure of the past and restore – perhaps in an even nobler form, at any rate in a more permanent one – the relation between art and the public that had once existed in Athens. I set down my thoughts in an essay entitled *Art and Revolution;* I originally intended it as the first of a series of articles to be published in a French newspaper, but I gave up the idea when it was pointed out to me that the period (the essay was written in 1849) was not a suitable one in which to address the Parisian public on such a topic. Today it is myself who feels that it would be out of place to trouble you further with the details of that libellous piece: I should be carried too far afield, and I am sure you will thank me for sparing you. For my purpose it is enough to have indicated the apparently remote regions to which I was drawn in the endeavour to find a basis for my artistic ideals – a basis in what was itself no more than an idealized reality.

I then turned to a subject which absorbed me for a longer time: the cause of that lamentable degeneration of ancient Greek drama. What struck me first of all was the manner in which the individual art forms that had combined to produce perfect drama dissolved and separated. Together, serving an end in common, they had been able to present the sublimest and deepest human truths to the understanding of the whole people. Now they went their separate ways, no longer inspired public preceptors but a consoling diversion for individual art-lovers: while the crowd regaled itself with gladiatorial shows and fights with animals, the cultivated few pursued the arts of literature and painting in seclusion. Especially important was the realisation – so it seemed to me – that these separate arts, however greatly their power and range were subsequently extended by men of genius, could never by themselves match the supremacy they had once achieved in combination without becoming unnatural and indeed false. Bearing in mind the findings of the most important art critics – for example, the investigations of Lessing into the boundaries between painting and poetry – I drew the conclusion that each of the arts tends to stretch its capacities to the limit, but cannot in the end transcend these limits without running the risk of becoming incomprehensible, fantastic and even absurd. At this point I seemed to behold how each branch of art longed for the helping hand of another related art, which alone could supply it. In view of my ideal it would naturally have interested me very much to trace the tendency in each separate branch; nevertheless, poetry's relation to music seemed to provide the most clearcut and (in view of the extraordinary importance of the latest musical trends) most striking example. By attempting to visualize a work of art which would unite all the single arts, allowing each to attain its highest perfection therein, I was led at last to formulate consciously the ideal, which had been gradually taking shape in my subconscious mind, as the answer to my artistic needs. Regarding as I did the realization of that ideal as an impossibility in the theatre as at present constituted, I entitled it *The Art-Work of the Future*. Under this title I published a still lengthier essay elaborating the above-indicated line of thought, and it was this (I might mention in passing) which evoked that spectre of a 'music of the future' which has been popularized and bruited around in French newspapers. You will now easily see from what misunderstandings the epithet arose and for what purposes it was invented.

Of this essay, too, I will spare you any detailed description, honoured friend! Its only value, I imagine, is for those who might not find it uninteresting to learn how, and in what manner, a creative artist once strove, primarily for his own sake, to reach solutions of problems usually handled only by professional critics, in whose eyes they could hardly have the same peculiar urgency. Likewise I will only give you a general outline of a third, still more extensive writing, published shortly after the last-mentioned under the title of *Opera and Drama*, since I cannot but suppose that its minutely detailed exposition of my main thought must have been more interesting to myself than it could ever be to others, either now or in the future. They were intimate meditations which, owing to my uncommonly lively interest in the subject, assumed in part a polemical character. What I did was to conduct a more searching investigation of the relationship between poetry and music in the specific context of dramatic art.

Here I felt bound above all to expose the fallacy of those who claimed that the ideal had been directly anticipated, if not yet attained, in opera as it already existed. Already in Italy, and still more so in France and in Germany, the topic had exercised brilliant minds. The conflict in Paris between the Gluckists and Piccinists was essentially a controversy – in the nature of the case an indecisive one – about whether the ideal of drama was attainable in opera. Those who held that it *was* attainable were, despite their apparent victory, seriously checked when their opponents brought up the counter-argument that in opera music played the dominant role, since it alone, not the poetry, was the guarantee of success. Voltaire, who in theory inclined to the former view, was compelled by this practical argument to deliver his damaging pronouncement: 'Ce qui est trop sot pour être dit, on le chante'. In Germany, Schiller and Goethe, stimulated by Lessing, considered the problem and came to build high hopes on opera – but then Goethe involuntarily confirmed the truth of Voltaire's pronouncement by an action which was in striking contrast to his own theoretical views: he himself wrote a number of operatic librettos and felt it necessary, in order to keep to the level of the *genre*, to make them as trivial as possible, in content as in execution. Indeed, it is with regret that we see these insipid pieces included among his collected poems.

I found it highly illuminating that brilliant minds should so often have entertained these hopes without them ever having been fulfilled. On the one hand it implied that the highest in drama might be attainable through a complete fusion of poetry and music. On the other hand it pointed to the fundamental defect of opera, a defect which in the nature of the case a musician would not be conscious of and which would also escape the attention of the poet. From the point of view of a poet who was not himself

'Music of the Future'

a musician, an opera was a firmly carpentered framework of musical forms that imposed specific rules for the invention and execution of the dramatic material he supplied. These forms only the musician could alter; and as to their content the poet commissioned to supply the libretto soon, without meaning to, exposed its worth in that he found himself obliged to degrade both his subject and his poetry to the level of triviality castigated in that pronouncement of Voltaire. In point of fact it is not necessary to lay bare the awkwardness, superficiality, not to say absurdity, of an operatic libretto; even in France the best efforts have been designed rather to conceal the evil than to remedy it. And so poets have always regarded the operatic form as a strange untouchable object to which they must perforce submit – which is why, apart from a few unfortunate exceptions, truly great poets have always steered clear of it.

At this point one asks oneself how musicians could have possibly attached an ideal significance to opera, when the poets engaged in it could not even meet the demands of a reasonably competent play – and when the musicians themselves, solely occupied with the development of purely musical forms, regarded opera as nothing more than a parade ground for the exercise of their specific talents. In the first part of *Opera and Drama* I took pains to expose the contradictoriness and perversity of what one expected the composer to achieve in such circumstances. I expressed my deep admiration for the overwhelmingly beautiful achievements of the great masters in this field; and when I pointed out weaknesses, there was no question of my trying to diminish their great reputation, since I could show that these flaws were all due to the defectiveness of the *genre* itself. The purpose of that demonstration – in itself distressing – was to drive home the argument that the ideal of a perfect opera, entertained by so many brilliant minds, could only be realized by a complete transformation of the poet's role.

In order to show that this role might be played freely and spontaneously, I gave special consideration to those hopes, repeatedly and insistently expressed by great poets and already mentioned above, of developing opera into an ideal *genre*. I sought to account for this and suggested that it was due to the poet's natural longing – affecting both the conception and the form of his poetry – to employ words, the material of abstract thought, in such a way as to arouse feeling. Obviously this affects his choice of subject: in what is termed a poetic view of life rationally explicable motives give way to motives actuated by purely human feeling. Likewise it affects a poem's form and diction. The poet's handling of words subordinates their abstract conventional meaning to their elemental sensuous quality: through the organization of metre and quasi-musical embellishment of rhyme his phraseology acquires a magical power of evoking and determining feeling. In this tendency, inherent in his very nature, we see the poet being drawn to the frontiers of his art and brought into direct contact with music; from which it follows that we must say of his poetry that at its best it would in its final consummation become completely music.

As the poet's ideal subject matter I felt bound to single out *myth*, that original, anonymously created poem of the people which throughout the ages, in one cultural period after another, great poets have treated in ever fresh ways. For here all that smacks of convention and all that pertains to abstract reason is completely missing: all we have is the eternally comprehensible, the purely human, albeit presented in that inimitably individual concrete form which is immediately recognizable in every genuine myth. The second part of my book dealt with this topic and led on to the question of the form of presentation best suited to this ideal subject matter.

In the book's third part I investigated the technical possibilities of that form. The conclusion I reached was that there was only one way of fulfilling these possibilities, namely, *through the uncommonly rich development, unknown to previous centuries, which music has undergone in our time.*

So deeply convinced am I of the importance of this statement that I cannot but regret that the opportunity to substantiate it is denied me here. I did so in my book – at any rate to my own satisfaction. If I attempt here to give you a brief outline, please take my word for it that what may strike you as paradoxical is at least gone into more thoroughly there.

It is undeniable that since the rebirth of the fine arts in Christian Europe two branches of art have undergone a development to which there is no parallel in classical antiquity; I refer to painting and music. The ideal significance of painting in the first century of the Renaissance is so well known and the characteristics of that wonderful period so well established that all we need to point out here is that it was something new in the history of art and belongs quite specifically to the modern world. To a greater and, to my mind, even more significant extent, the same could be said of modern music. The element of harmony was completely unknown to the ancients, and its inconceivably rich expansion through polyphony is the peculiar creation of recent centuries.

The only Greek music we know of is that which accompanied dancing. Its rhythm, and that of the poem sung to the dance tune, was governed by dance movements, and so strictly were verse and melody governed by this rhythm that Greek music (the term almost always included poetry) can be thought of as dancing articulated through tones and words. It was those living dance tunes – originally associated with pagan rites and embodying the essence of all antique music – which the early Christian communes took over and gradually absorbed into their own religious services. In this solemn ceremony dancing was forbidden as worldly and godless, which meant that the essential element in antique music, its uncommonly vital and varied rhythm, was lost; and melody was left with the completely unaccented rhythms which characterize the chorales still sung in our churches today.

The loss of rhythmic vitality obviously deprived the melody of its distinctive expressive function. How little of that was left we can judge for ourselves by imagining such a melody without any supporting harmony. It was in order to heighten the expression inherent in melody itself that the Christian mind invented four-part harmony on the basis of the four-part chord, whose characteristic mutations would henceforth motivate the expression as formerly the rhythm had done. Thereby the melodic phrase did indeed attain a wonderful expressiveness, a depth, an intimacy never before known – as witness the incomparable masterpieces of Italian church music, which move us afresh whenever we hear them. Here we find voices, originally employed merely to provide the melody's supporting harmony, manipulated in a free, continuously expressive development; through the so-called art of counterpoint each voice could be employed independently and expressively beneath the melody proper (the so-called *cantus firmus*): hence it is that a performance of the choral works of those revered masters moves us to the depths of our being in a way no other art is capable of.

The rise of operatic melody which took place in Italy as this art declined I can only regard as a relapse into paganism. As the church declined the demand for secular music grew, and this demand was most easily met by reviving melody's original rhythmic quality and applying it to song as it had been done previously to dance. The striking incongruity between modern verse, developed on the pattern of Christian melody, and this imposed dance-melody is a topic I shall not enter into; it will suffice to point out that dance-melody paid very little attention to the verse and that eventually its variations and divisions were dictated exclusively by virtuosos. In any case, the chief reason for regarding the rise of dance-melody as a relapse rather than an advance is its glaring inability to make use of those two all-important creations of Christian music: harmony and a harmony-embodying polyphony. The harmonic basis of Italian operatic melody was so obvious that it could at times dispense with any accompaniment at all, and for the arrangement of its sections it made do with a periodic structure so impoverished that the cultivated musician of today looks back with pained astonishment on those paltry, almost childish forms whose narrow limits would bring even the greatest composer to a standstill, were he to handle them.

In Germany, on the other hand, the secularization of church music gave rise to an important new development. The German masters also went back to the primitive rhythmic melody which had lived on among the people as a national dance-form; but instead of dispensing with the rich harmony of ecclesiastical music, they sought to unite it with the rhythmically animated melody in order that rhythm and harmony should participate in the melody's expression. They employed their contrapuntal skill not only to preserve the independent movement of the polyphonic voices, but to make each single voice a carrier of the melody; thus whereas formerly the melody was confined to the *cantus firmus*, now each accompanying part delivered it. Whoever has had the good fortune to hear one of Bach's choral works worthily performed will know what an incredibly diversified, enthralling effect – an effect peculiar to music – is created when lyrical impulse is imparted to rhythmic melody in this manner: I have in mind especially Bach's eight-part motet *Singet dem Herrn ein neues Lied*, where the lyrical impulse of the rhythmic melody seems to surge through an ocean of harmonic waves.

In German instrumental music the development of rhythmic melody on a foundation of Christian harmony culminated in an even greater freedom and led to an expressiveness of the utmost subtlety and variety.

The aspect to which in this context I would like to draw your attention is the formal expansion of the primitive dance-melody. The independent treatment of the various voices as developed in vocal church music spread after the emergence of the string quartet to the full orchestra and emancipated it from the humble role it had hitherto performed – and which it still does in Italian opera – of merely supplying a rhythmic and harmonic accompaniment. It is highly interesting, and in a study of musical form uniquely illuminating, to observe how the German masters concentrated all their efforts upon imparting a richer and broader development to the simple dance-melody when played as a purely independent piece. The dance-melody was originally a short four-bar period which could be doubled or quadrupled, and it seems to have been the fundamental aim of those masters to extend this period in order to make possible a richer development of harmony. The artistic device of fugue, applied to dance-melody, made for a longer duration in that it enabled voices to deliver the melody in diverse ways: diminished or augmented; reflected in the shifting light of modulation; enlivened by counter-themes and contrapuntal figures. Another procedure was to line up a succession of melodies, with an eye to the effect of their alternating expression, and to link them by means of transitions, in which contrapuntal skill was of especial value. It was upon this simple basis that the symphony was built. Haydn was the first great master to expand the form and give it a deep expressive significance through the inexhaustible wealth of his themes, transition passages and developments.

Meanwhile the melody of Italian opera was still making do with its meagre formal structure: nevertheless, in the mouth of the gifted, sensitive singer, sustained by the vocal chords of the noblest of musical instruments, it had a sensuous charm which the instrumental melodies of the German masters lacked. It was Mozart who became aware of this magic and, by applying the more advanced techniques of German instrumental composition to Italian opera, imparted the full euphony of the Italian vocal style to orchestral melody. The heritage of these two masters, so richly promising, then passed to Beethoven, in whose hands the symphonic art attained a gripping breadth of form and a melodic content of such unheard-of variety that the Beethoven symphony appears to us today as a milestone in the history of art. It has brought into the world something the like of which has never been known before in the art of any period or people.

No one had ever heard before such a language as that spoken by the instruments of a Beethoven symphony. The listener is riveted by a purely musical expression of unprecedented length and inconceivably manifold nuances; with a power no other art can equal it stirs his inmost being. And this language is governed by an ordering principle of such freedom and daring that the principle seems more powerful than any logic we know of, and this even though logical laws seem not in the slightest involved – indeed, rational thinking, governed by relations of cause and effect, appear to have no foothold on it whatsoever. Such a symphony, therefore, cannot but have the appearance of a revelation from another world. In truth, it does relate the phenomena of the world to each other in a way completely different from the normal laws of logic. Certainly it is a revelation which impresses itself upon us with such conviction and determines our emotions so unerringly that in the face of it logical thinking is confounded and disarmed.

That this completely novel language should have been discovered in precisely our age I regard as a metaphysical necessity imposed by the increasingly conventional development of modern speech. When we consider the history of modern languages more closely, we still find an origin in the so-called word-roots, which clearly reveal that initially the conceptualization of objects was almost entirely bound up with subjective feeling. Thus to assume that Man's first language originally bore a close resemblance to song is perhaps not utterly ridiculous. In any case it was out of words, whose significance was grasped in a purely sensuous, subjective way, that language evolved, and this evolution became more and more abstract, with the result that eventually words were left with only a conventional meaning, in the understanding of which feeling played no part, their arrangement and structure being made entirely dependent on learnt rules. Concomitant with the evolution of morals in human society, both manners and language inevitably became subject to conventions of which the rules were no longer grasped by natural feeling, but imposed by maxims of education that had to be imbibed. Yet while the languages of modern Europe and their many sub-divisions were becoming more and more obviously subject to convention, the art of music was evolving a capacity for expression such as the world had never known. It is as though purely human feeling had been driven by the oppression of conventional civilization to seek an outlet for the assertion of its own peculiar laws of speech, an outlet through which it could make itself understood untramelled by the rules of logical thinking. The extraordinary popularity of music in our time; the increasing interest in music of a serious kind spreading through all layers of society; the growing eagerness to have music treated as an essential part of our children's education – these indisputable developments add weight to the view that modern music has evolved in answer to a deep need, and that, if its language is inaccessible to laws of logic, this is because it makes a more compelling appeal to our comprehension than those laws themselves.

In the face of all this two and only two paths of development lie open to poetry. Either it gives itself over entirely to abstraction, to pure combinations of mental concepts and interpretations of the world by explaining the logical laws of thought – and this it does as philosophy. Or it effects an intimate union with music – that is to say, with the sort of music whose infinite power has been revealed through the symphonies of Beethoven.

Poetry will find this path and acknowledge its own deep longing for an eventual merging with music as soon as it realizes that music itself has a need which only poetry can fulfil. To explain this need we have to remind ourselves of the human mind's ineradicable impulse, when confronted by an impressive phenomenon, to put the question: Why? Even when we are listening to a symphony the question cannot be completely suppressed and, since the symphony is least of all able to provide an answer, the question puts the listener's perceptual faculties, bound to the laws of causality, into a state of confusion. This not only has the effect of disturbing him, it also gives rise to an entirely false judgment.

Only a poet can provide this disturbing, yet inescapable question with an answer which would, as it were, by circumvention prevent it from ever being put. But, again, the only poet who can do this is one who is intimately aware of music's inexhaustible expressive power and who accordingly so frames his poem that it may penetrate to the finest threads of the musical tissue and dissolve its spoken thoughts entirely into feeling.

Obviously the only poetic form that would serve is one in which the poet does not merely describe his subject, but presents it in direct living terms – that is to say, in the form of drama. Drama, through its scenic representation of an action imitating real life as faithfully as possible, instantaneously arouses in the audience a feeling of intimate participation, and this participation induces a state of ecstasy in which that momentous 'Why?' is forgotten and one willingly abandons oneself to the guidance of those new laws which enable music to make itself so miraculously comprehensible, those laws which – in a profound sense – provide the only right answer to that 'Why?'.

In the third part of the above-mentioned essay I attempted to deal more closely with the technical principles involved in bringing about this intimate union of music with poetry in drama. You will not, I am sure, expect me to recapitulate them here: I do not doubt that the above outline of my fundamental position has fatigued you no less than it has done me – indeed from my own fatigue I realise that I have been involuntarily working myself into something like the condition I was in when I wrote that theoretical work years ago, a condition in which my brain was so strangely and morbidly oppressed – I described it above as abnormal – that I recoil from the prospect of falling into it again.

I called that condition abnormal because I was under a compulsion to treat as a theoretical problem what I had come to feel absolutely certain about from an artistic standpoint; I had to make it completely clear to my reflective consciousness and so abstract contemplation was necessary. To an artist nothing is more alien and repugnant than that kind of thinking, so utterly opposed to the usual nature of his own. He cannot bring to it the required calm composure of the professional theoretician; rather, he is impelled by a passionate impatience which prevents him from giving the necessary time and attention to matters of style; he wants to put into every sentence the picture of the whole that is constantly in his mind; he doubts whether he has succeeded and the doubt drives him to make the attempt again, so that eventually he works himself into a state of irritation and excitement completely unknown to the theoretician. Aware of all the error and failure, and upset still further by his awareness of it, he hurriedly finishes off his work, telling himself with a sigh that when all is said and done he can only expect to be understood by one who already shares his artistic standpoint.

My condition, then, was a kind of cramp: I was straining to formulate theoretically what I could not communicate in the infallible form of a convincing work of art owing to the disparity between my outlook and the one generally held concerning the present state of opera. From this painful condition I then returned to the normal exercise of my artistic faculties. I sketched and carried out the plan of a drama on a scale so large that the subject compelled me deliberately to repudiate all possibility of its being incorporated in the existing opera repertoire. This music drama encompassing an entire tetralogy could only be brought to performance under the most exceptional conditions. This ideal prospect, cutting me off completely from the whole field of modern opera, so flattered my imagination and raised my spirits that, bothering no more about cranky theories and immersing myself in prolonged artistic creation, I returned to my natural element like one recovering from a serious illness. The work I am referring to – the greater part of which I have finished, and this includes the musical composition – is called *Der Ring des Nibelungen*. If the present attempt to provide you with prose translations of my opera texts meets with your approval perhaps I will arrange to provide such a translation of the text of that cycle.

So, by resigning myself to no further contact with the artistic world while carrying out my plans, I recovered from the trials of my painful expedition into the realms of speculative theory. And I resolved that no provocation – not even the most idiotic of the many misunderstandings my theoretical writings have given rise to – would ever tempt me into those realms again. Meanwhile a development was taking place in my relation to the artistic world which I had not in the least expected.

My operas – one of which (*Lohengrin*) I had never heard and the other only when I myself was in charge of their performance – had been spreading all over Germany enjoying an ever increasing success and finally a lasting popularity. Though at bottom this surprised me, it reinforced the observation I had often made during my former working career – and it was this which had kept me bound to the operatic theatre for all that it repelled me – namely, that exceptional performances did sometimes occur and that the richness of their achievement and the effects they produced revealed to me possibilities which, as I have already mentioned, induced me to formulate my ideals. Since I did not attend any of those performances of my operas I could judge of their character only from the reports of perceptive friends and from their success with the public. My friends' reports gave me no reason to suppose they were above the average. This confirmed me in my pessimism – all the same, when something really good, even excellent, was achieved I enjoyed the pessimist's advantage of being able to rejoice all the more heartily because I had not expected it and had done nothing to further it – whereas in former days, when I was an optimist, I regarded goodness and excellence, because they were possible, as imperative standards and was accordingly intolerant and ungrateful. Those reports of occasional, unexpectedly fine

'Music of the Future'

achievements filled me with a fresh warmth and gratitude. Previously I had held that such achievements depended on a properly ordered condition of society; now I accepted that they were, after all, possible as exceptions.

Almost more important than this, though, was the observation that the public received my works with extraordinary enthusiasm even when their performance was highly questionable, indeed often positively distorted. When I think how bitterly those operas were attacked by critics to whom my theoretical writings were anathema and who stubbornly assumed that the composition of the operas, even though they dated from an earlier period, had been arbitrarily determined by the said theories – when I think of this, I cannot but regard the public's enthusiasm for my works as a highly important, encouraging sign. That the public when, as happened in Germany, they heard the critics crying: 'Turn away from Rossini's siren strains, close your eyes to those tinsel melodies!' should ignore the critics, because they enjoyed listening to the melodies – that is understandable. But here you have critics continually telling people not to waste their money on a thing that could not possibly give them any pleasure, telling them that what they go to the opera for – namely, melodies – are conspicuous by their absence and that instead they will find nothing but the most boring recitative together with an utterly incomprehensible musical rigmarole – in short, 'Music of the Future!'.

Imagine, then, my reaction when, as well as irrefutable evidence of a genuine popular success among the German public as a whole, I received personal testimonies of a complete change of outlook from people who had hitherto only taken pleasure in the lascivious side of opera and ballet, and who had contemptuously rejected the notion of an art combining music and drama that deserved to be taken seriously! I have received not a few such testimonies – allow me to explain just why I found them so deeply encouraging and so consoling.

Obviously the question of my talent, whether great or small, was not the issue: not even my most hostile critics attacked me on that ground. What they objected to was my outlook; my success they sought to explain by declaring that my talent was superior to my outlook. Unmoved by that so flattering declaration I could now enjoy the satisfaction of knowing that my instinct had been right when I reckoned that the mutual saturation of poetry and music, when actually realised on the stage, would create an impression of irresistible power, an impression that would cause all conscious reflection to be dissolved into purely human feeling. The knowledge that this could be achieved even when the performance – a matter to which I attach such importance – was grossly inadequate led me to form still bolder views regarding the all-encompassing power of music. These views I must now finally endeavour to explain.

I can only hope to express myself clearly on this difficult, yet so important, topic if I concentrate on the aspect of form to the exclusion of everything else. In my theoretical works I also attempted to deal with music's content, but since in the nature of the case I could only do so in the abstract I ran the risk of being totally incomprehensible, or at any rate misunderstood. For this reason, as I have already said, nothing on earth will induce me, even in this communication to you, to undertake anything of that sort again. Nevertheless I realise how misleading it is to talk about a form without giving any idea of its content. As I confessed in my opening paragraph, it was only your request for a translation of my opera texts that nerved me to attempt to describe my theoretical methods so far as I have become conscious of them. Let me therefore now say a brief word about those texts; it will then, I hope, be possible to confine my remarks to the subject of musical form which is especially important in this context and has given rise to so many wrong ideas.

First of all, though, I must ask you to excuse my having sent you these texts only in a prose translation. The endless difficulty we had translating the verses of *Tannhäuser* – shortly to be staged before the Parisian public – makes it clear that to attempt to do likewise with the other texts would take more time than I can allow at present. I shall have to dispense with the effect of the poetry and be satisfied if the subjects of the dramas and the way I have treated them convey an idea of the role which music played in the conception and shaping of the whole. I trust this purpose will be served by translations whose sole merit is that they render the words of the original as faithfully as possible.

The first three of these works – *The Flying Dutchman*, *Tannhäuser* and *Lohengrin* – were already conceived, composed and, with the exception of *Lohengrin*, produced before I wrote my theoretical essays. It would be possible (if this could be done by referring only to their subjects) to demonstrate by means of these operas the course of my artistic development up to the point when I felt obliged to provide a theoretical justification of my methods. But I only mention this in order to remind you how mistaken it is to suppose that these three works were deliberately composed according to pre-conceived abstract rules. The truth of the matter is that the most daring of my theoretical speculations concerning the form of music drama were brewing within me precisely because at that very time I was carrying in my head the plan of my great Nibelung drama (some of the text of which I had already written). Thus my theories were virtually little more than an abstract expression of the artistic process then at work within me. My system, if you want to call it that, you will find only to a very limited extent reflected in those first three texts.

'Music of the Future'

But with the last text I am submitting to you, *Tristan and Isolde*, the case is otherwise. It was conceived and carried out after the greater part of the Nibelung pieces had been set to music. I had a practical reason for interrupting my great work: the desire to produce a simpler, more performable piece, on a smaller scale, making fewer scenic demands. Behind this lay the longing to hear a work of mine again, and those consoling performances of my early works in Germany, of which I have already written, encouraged me to believe that now my desire could be realized. This work I should permit to be judged according to the strictest demands based on my theories – not because I wrote it to any system – by this time I had completely forgotten all theory – but because here at last I was able to proceed with such complete freedom and disregard of all theoretical considerations that while writing it I was myself aware that I was going far beyond my own system. Believe me, there is no greater bliss than the artist's unthinking sense of absolute certainty which I experienced when I was creating *Tristan*. Perhaps what made it possible was that I had been fortified by a previous period of reflection – fortified in rather the same way that that teacher of mine had foretold when he declared that a stringent course of counterpoint would help me not to write fugues, but to achieve what was only possible through hard exercise: independence, confidence...!

Let me now briefly call to mind the opera that preceded *The Flying Dutchman* – *Rienzi*, a work full of youthful fire, which brought me my first success in Germany: as well as my other operas it is still continually performed not only at Dresden, where it was first produced, but at many other theatres. Its conception and formal lay-out reflect the heroic opera of Spontini and the brilliant Parisian Grand Opéra *genre* of Auber, Meyerbeer and Halévy which in my early days I strove to emulate. I attach little importance to it now since it contains no essential trace of my subsequent development; in any case it is not in order to present myself as a successful opera composer that I am raising the topic, but in order to explain a problematic aspect of my development. This *Rienzi* of mine was completed during my first stay in Paris; before my eyes was the brilliant Grand Opéra and I flattered myself with the presumptuous idea of seeing it produced there. Should this youthful wish one day be fulfilled, I am sure you would agree with me that the ways of fate are very strange – to introduce such a lengthy time-gap between wish and fulfilment and to fill that gap with experiences of such a completely different nature!

Directly after *Rienzi*, which was planned on the largest scale in five acts, came *The Flying Dutchman*, which I originally intended to be performed in only one act. As you can see, the lure of the Parisian ideal had faded; I began to draw my formal principles from another source than the surrounding ocean of publicly approved music-making. What my mood was you can judge for yourself: the text clearly expresses it. Whether this text has any literary value I do not know; what I do know is that when I was writing it I did not feel as I did when framing the words for *Rienzi*, when all I had in mind was a 'libretto' that would enable me to fill out as richly as possible the requisite grand-operatic forms: introductions, finales, choruses, arias, duets, terzets and the like.

In *The Flying Dutchman* and in all my subsequent works I turned my back on history and drew my material from the realm of saga. I will leave aside here the inner motives for that decision and instead dwell upon a single aspect: the influence of the choice of material upon the shaping of the poetic and, in particular, the musical form.

It meant that I could dispense with all those conventional descriptive details of a past epoch that a historic subject must have if the plot is to be properly followed – all those details which the novelists and dramatic poets of our day so amply supply. Thereby the poem and the music would be relieved of a function alien to the nature of both, and in the case of music a sheer impossibility. For a saga, whatever period and nation it may derive from, has the merit that what it seizes upon is the purely human aspect of a period and nation and does this in a way peculiar to itself, pregnant, immediately understandable. Any ballad or popular folk song bears striking witness to this. Furthermore the legendary atmosphere imparted to the presentation of a purely human event has the merit of greatly lightening that task which I assigned to the poet of circumventing the question 'Why?' The character of the scene, the legendary tone, transport the mind into a dream-like state which soon becomes a clairvoyant vision: the phenomena of the world are then perceived as possessing a coherence they do not have for the inquiring mind in its ordinary waking state, forever asking 'Why?' in order to overcome its fear of the incomprehensible world – that world it now perceives so clearly and vividly. How music should consummate the magic of this clairvoyant vision you will readily understand. . . .

From the poet's point of view a legendary subject has another essential dramatic advantage. Not only does the simple, easily grasped action spare him the necessity of retarding explanations; it provides the greatest possible scope for revealing those inner psychic motives which alone can bring home the inevitability of the action since we ourselves feel them in our own hearts.

When you yourself look over the texts you will observe that it was only gradually that I became conscious of this advantage and learnt to exploit it. The increasing length of each successive work is one indication: you will soon realize that my original reluctance to develop a poem on a broader scale was due to my still having had in mind the traditional forms of operatic music, for which a text was unthinkable that did not contain a mass of verbal repetition. In *The Flying Dutchman* I was only concerned in a general way to preserve the simplest features of the action by getting rid of all pointless detail relating to an intrigue of everyday life. This left me free to deal more broadly with those general features which appeared to present the saga's characteristic atmosphere in the proper light since they completely coincided with the action's psychic motives; that is to say, it left me free to deal with them in such a way that that very atmosphere would itself become the action.

Already you will perhaps find *Tannhäuser* to a much greater extent developed out of inner motives. The decisive catastrophe arises naturally out of the lyrical song-competition, where no other force than a hidden psychic feeling decides the issue, and that in such a way that the decision itself is presented in a purely lyrical way. The whole interest of *Lohengrin* lies in an experience taking place in the heart of Elsa which reaches down to the mind's very depths. The blissful spell, which casts its magic so convincingly over the whole setting, can last only so long as she does not ask where it comes from. The question bursts forth like a cry from the troubled depths of her womanly heart – and the spell is broken. It will not escape you how singularly that tragic 'Whence?' coincides with that theoretical 'Why?' referred to above.

As I have explained, I myself was driven to put questions which for a long time broke the spell of my art. The painful price I paid taught me to stop questioning. I was free of all doubts when at last I threw myself into *Tristan*. Completely confident, I immersed myself in the depths of the psyche and from this inmost centre of the world boldly constructed an external form. You have only to glance at the voluminous text and you will see at once that, whereas the writer of a historical text is obliged to give a detailed exposition of the external events of his plot obscuring any revelation of its inner motives, in my case the detailed exposition is of just those motives and only those. Life and death, the import and existence of the external world here depend entirely upon inner psychic events. The whole affecting story is the outcome of a soul's inmost need, and it comes to light as reflected from within.

Maybe you will think that the poem contains far too much in the way of intimate detail; while not objecting to intimate details as such, you may wonder how a poet could dare to give them to a musician to transcribe. Were this so, you would be experiencing the same timidity which led me when I was conceiving *The Flying Dutchman* to give the text only broad general contours of a kind that should lend themselves to purely musical treatment. Of one thing, though, I must assure you, namely, that whereas the verses of *The Flying Dutchman* were written with operatic melody in mind and contain numerous repetitions of words and phrases in order to give that melody the requisite breadth, *Tristan* contains no verbal repetitions whatsoever. Instead you have a web of words and verses prescribing in advance the whole lay-out of the melody; that is to say, here the melody is already poetically predetermined.

You would have to agree, I think, that were such a procedure successful it would lead far more than my former one to an intimate blending of poetry with music. And if, as I hope, you regard the text I have written for *Tristan* as superior to my previous ones, then you would have to conclude that at any rate it was all the better for having fulfilled the function of predetermining the musical form. But if the poem *qua* poem may have gained, the question arises whether the music has not suffered, whether it has not been deprived of the freedom it needs for movement and development?

To this I will reply as a musician and deliver the answer which I know in my heart of hearts to be true: the procedure I have been describing gives the melody and its form a wealth and inexhaustibility which would otherwise be utterly impossible.

I cannot do better that round off this communication by providing you with a theoretical justification for that answer. I will attempt this by concentrating at last solely upon the musical form, the melody.

Those shrill cries for 'melody, melody!' so often raised nowadays by the superficial dilettanti in our midst only serve to convince me that their conception of melody is drawn from works where, along with melody, you have a dearth of melody which makes the melody they cry for so very precious. In Italy the public goes to the opera for an evening's entertainment; the music sung on the stage is part of the entertainment; from time to time, when conversation is broken off, it is listened to; the music continues throughout the visits people pay each other in their boxes fulfilling the function of background music at grand dinners, namely, that of stimulating shy guests to converse more freely. Such music virtually comprises the whole score of an Italian opera: the portion that is actually listened to probably amounts to no more than a twelfth. An opera must contain at least one aria worth attending to; a really successful one would have to be capable of stopping the conversation at least half a dozen times. A composer capable of stopping it as many as a dozen times would be hailed as an inexhaustible melodic genius. Imagine such an audience suddenly confronted with a work every bar of which demanded the same amount of attention throughout its entire length! You couldn't blame it for feeling rudely torn out of its normal listening habits – how could it possibly be expected to recognise its beloved 'melody' in a thing which at its best could hardly be considered more than a refinement of that musical noise which in its simpler form serves the purpose of promoting pleasant conversation? And, what is more, this stuff positively demands to be listened to! The audience would clamour for the restoration of its six to twelve melodies in order to be sure of having time for the conversation which is the evening's chief purpose.

What has the appearance of wealth to some tastes looks poverty-stricken to others. One can pardon the general public its error, but not the critics. So far as possible, therefore, let us look into this error and see what it involves.

It must be affirmed at the outset that *melody is the only form of music* – that music without melody is unthinkable, that the two are absolutely inseparable. To say that a piece of music has no melody is in a higher sense tantamount to saying that the composer has failed to create a form that grips and stirs our emotions; and that this is so because his lack of talent and originality has forced him to fall back on hackneyed melodic phrases that make no impact. Delivered by an uncultivated opera-goer, though, such a judgment would refer only to melody of that specific, narrow type, touched on above, belonging to the childhood of the art – for which reason the exclusive pleasure taken in it actually does seem childish. What is involved here is not so much true melody as melody in its limited original pure *dance-form*.

Not that I wish to say anything derogatory about that original basis of melodic form. I have sought to show that it underlies the consummate form of the Beethoven symphony and this in itself is sufficiently impressive. It must be borne in mind, though, that while in Italian opera the form has remained in its original undeveloped state, in the Beethoven symphony it has been so expanded and cultivated that its relation to the original can be likened to that of a flowering plant to a tiny shoot. Following the precept that a form, be it never so developed, must retain something of its original state if it is to remain comprehensible, I detect the presence of this dance-form in the Beethoven symphony – indeed I regard the Beethoven symphony, considered as a melodic entity, as nothing other than idealized dance-form.

Here we must observe that this form is spread over every part of the symphony – in sharp contrast to the melodies of Italian opera which are isolated, the intervening spaces being filled by music which we must call unmelodic since it scarcely rises above the level of mere noise. In Beethoven's predecessors, even in symphonic movements, you still find awkward spaces between principal melodic motives: Haydn usually managed to make his transition-passages very interesting and significant; Mozart kept closer to the Italian model – time and again, one might almost say as a general rule, he falls back upon stereotyped phrases giving his movements the character of background music providing an attractive noise to accompany conversations between attractive melodies – at least, that is how those perpetually recurring, pompously fussy half-closes in Mozart's symphonies strike me; it is just as though the music were expressing the rattle and clatter of a princely dinner. Beethoven, supreme genius that he was, so managed matters that those fatal intermediate passages completely disappear: his principal melodic motives are linked by music which itself possesses to the full the character of melody.

To go into this more closely would be extremely interesting but would carry me too far afield. All the same, I cannot resist drawing your attention to the structure of a Beethoven first movement. What we see is a dance-melody split into its tiniest fragments, each one of which – it may amount to no more than a couple of notes – is made interesting and significant by a pervasive rhythm or significant harmony. The fragments are continually being reassembled in different formations – coalescing in a logical succession which here pours forth like a stream, there disperses as though in a whirlwind. Throughout one is riveted by their vivid expressiveness, absorbed by the excitement of sensing melodic significance in every harmony, even in every rest. And the outcome, never before achieved, of this procedure was the expansion of a melody, through the richly varied development of all the motives it contained, into a continuous large-scale piece, which in itself constituted a single, perfectly coherent melody.

It is a striking fact that although German masters have carried this essentially instrumental technique quite far in music for choir and orchestra, they have as yet never made any real use of it in opera. In his great Mass Beethoven handled his choir and orchestra very much as in a symphony: he could do this because the familiar symbolic words of the text provided, as dance-melody did, a given form which could be split up, repeated, reassembled etc. But no sensitive musician would dream of dealing in that way with the text of a drama, since here the words are no longer only symbolic; they must follow a definite logical sequence. But this of course only applies to texts written for the traditional forms of opera; it leaves open the possibility of a dramatic poem itself providing a counterpart to a symphonic form – a counterpart which, while completely meeting the demands of this rich form, would be in perfect conformity with the fundamental principles of drama.

Since this is a problem extremely difficult to explain theoretically, it would, I think, clarify matters if I were to present it in a metaphorical form.

'Music of the Future'

I have spoken of the symphony as the realization of the ideal of melodic dance-form. The minuet or scherzo of a Beethoven symphony is in fact a primitive dance music which could easily be danced to. It is as as though the composer felt an instinctive need to reach down just once to his work's foundations and, as it were, test with his feet the ground on which it was to be built. In the other movements melodies become less capable of being danced to; the dance would have to be of an ideal kind, no closer to the primitive dance than the symphony itself is to the primitive dance-melody. Perhaps this is why the composer maintains a certain reserve, keeps his musical expression within certain limits – that is to say, does not sound the note of tragic passion too strongly: emotions and expectations would be aroused compelling the listener to put that unsettling 'Why?' which the composer cannot satisfactorily answer.

The idealized form of dance that would exactly fit his music is in fact to be found in the *dramatic action*. This actually does bear the same relation to the primitive dance that a symphony does to a simple dance-tune: even folk-dancing in its original form conveyed a dramatic action, usually the wooing of a pair of lovers; when that simple representation of a sensual experience is developed into a revelation of its psychic impulses then you have a dramatic action. (That our modern ballet falls short of providing such a revelation is a topic you must allow me to pass over. Ballet is a fit mate for opera, reared on the same false basis; for which reason they cling together, each covering up the other's defects.)

A programme, which provokes rather than stills the impulse to put that disturbing question 'Why?', cannot convey the meaning of a symphony. This can only be done by a dramatic action depicted on the stage.

Since I have already set forth my grounds for this assertion, it now only remains to consider the matter from the point of view of melodic form and indicate how a truly complementary dramatic poem can give this form a fresh vitality and breadth. A poet who is fully aware of the inexhaustible expressive possibilities of symphonic melody will feel impelled to match in his own sphere the subtlest, most intimate nuances of that melody, which can stir us to the depths with a single harmonic shift. The narrow confining limits of 'operatic melody' will no longer cow him into providing a dull meaningless canvas. On the contrary, by watching the musician he will discover a secret the musician himself does not know – that melodic form is capable of an infinitely greater development than the symphony has so far made possible. Intuitively divining this development, he will anticipate it by designing his poem with the utmost freedom.

Thus the poet will say to the symphonist, who still clings timidly to the original dance form, not daring to push his mode of expression beyond its narrow limits: 'Plunge boldly into the sea of music; with my hand in yours you can never lose contact with the things that all men understand. For with my help you are in constant touch with the firm ground of a dramatic action, and the scenic representation of such an action is the most immediately understandable poem of all. Frame your melody boldly, so that it pours through the whole work like an uninterrupted stream; in it you will be voicing what I leave unsaid, for only you can say it; while I in my silence will still be saying it all, because it is your hand I am guiding.'

In truth, the measure of a poet's greatness is that which he does not say in order to let what is inexpressible speak to us for itself. It is the musician who brings this great Unsaid to sounding life, and the unmistakable form of his resounding silence is *endless melody*.

Necessarily it will be only through his own specific medium, the orchestra, that the symphonist will be able to frame this melody. Needless to say, he will employ it in a very different manner from that of the Italian opera composer in whose hands the orchestra merely accompanies the arias like a monstrous guitar.

In the drama as I conceive it the orchestra's relation to the stage action will be broadly comparable to that of the chorus of Greek tragedy. The chorus was present throughout, watching the motives of the unfolding action reveal themselves and endeavouring to fathom them and assess the drama in their light. But this participation was essentially reflective: the chorus itself stood apart both from the action and the theme. The modern symphony orchestra, on the other hand, will be intimately involved: it will embody the harmony which alone makes possible the melody's specific expression; it will maintain the melody in a state of uninterrupted flow so that the motives will be able to work with the maximum effect upon the audience's feelings. If we assume that the ideal work of art is that which can be grasped without reflection and through which the artist's vision speaks most clearly to the emotions; and if we can regard music drama as the art which ideally fulfils these conditions, then the symphony orchestra is the wonderful instrument that alone makes such a work of art possible. This means, of course, that the chorus, which already in opera had mounted the stage, would now entirely lose the function it had performed in ancient Greek drama. Henceforth it could only be employed as an active participant; if this were not possible then its presence would be disturbing and superfluous; for now its reflective role would be taken over by the orchestra which can perform it with an immediacy that never disturbs.

To give you a final idea of this great melody which I visualize spanning the whole compass of a music drama I shall again employ a metaphor. I am concerned here only with the impression this melody must make upon the listener. Its wealth of detail, branching out in infinitely many different directions, should be apparent not only to the expert but also to the naivest layman once he has attuned himself to listen. First of all, therefore, it must convey an impression rather like that which a beautiful forest makes upon the solitary visitor who comes there from the noisy city on a summer evening. The essence of that impression (the many and various feelings involved I must leave to the reader's imagination) is the sense of a silence becoming ever more eloquent. For the artist's purpose it suffices to create that fundamental first impression, and then, without the listener's being aware of it, to lead him on to higher things: he will unconsciously imbibe them of his own accord. When under the spell of that impression the listener seats himself and, liberated as he is from the noise of the city, perceives afresh, hears with new ears, listens ever more intently, he becomes increasingly aware of a multitude of voices in the forest – new ones keep on entering, each different and such as he had never heard before; they gather strength as they accumulate; louder and ever louder. . . . And yet, even though the voices are so numerous and the songs so various, the radiant, swelling tones only seem to be that single great forest melody which had first arrested him – just as the sight of the deep-blue night sky arrests him, and then the longer he loses himself in the spectacle the more clearly he perceives the multitude of dazzling stars. Afterwards the melody will be forever resounding in his mind, though he will never be able to hum it – to hear it again he must go back to the forest, and on a summer evening. What folly to think of catching one of those charming forest songsters and taking it home to have it warble a fragment of that great melody! What would he hear but – just that fragment whichever it might be?

You can well imagine what a great number of technical details I have had to pass over in this sketchy – and yet perhaps already too lengthy – account; but of course even in a theoretical exposition details of this nature are inexhaustible. In order to clarify all the different aspects of melodic form as I conceive them – its relation to operatic melody proper; its possibilities of expansion from the point of view of periodic structure and of harmony – I should have no alternative but to return to my previous, and fruitless, attempt. For this reason I prefer to confine myself to a general outline for the interested reader since, even in this communication, we are approaching the point where only the work itself can provide the full explanation.

You would be wrong in thinking that this last observation is a reference to the forthcoming Paris production of *Tannhäuser*. You have seen the score of *Tristan;* although I have no intention of putting it forward as the ideal model, nevertheless I think you will agree that the step I took from

Tannhäuser to *Tristan* was a far bigger one than that from my original operatic standpoint to *Tannhäuser*. Anyone who regards this communication purely and simply as a preparation for the performance of *Tannhäuser* is in for a considerable disappointment.

If I am afforded the pleasure of seeing my *Tannhäuser* winning the plaudits of the Parisian public too, I have no doubt its success will be largely due to the obvious connections it has with the operas of my predecessors, above all those of Weber. But I should like to indicate briefly the way in which even this early work of mine differs to some extent from previous operas.

It goes without saying that what I have been describing here as the strict consequence of an ideal procedure has always been implicit in the works of the great masters. It was by no means as the result of abstract reflection that I reached my conclusions, but as the result of conclusions drawn from my observation of the works of these masters. The great Gluck confronted a stiff narrow framework of operatic forms, which stood side by side, for the most part unconnected; he himself effected no fundamental change of principle, but step by step his successors brought together and expanded these forms, so that when the dramatic situation called for it they were perfectly capable of serving the highest purpose. I need not enumerate the many fine examples of music used for dramatic effect, as powerful as they are beautiful, which can be found in many works of the revered masters; nobody acknowledges them with more delight than I do. Even in the feebler works of frivolous composers I have discovered effects that astonish me and which give proof of the above-mentioned incomparable power of music – by virtue of the unassailable definiteness of melodic expression – to raise a singer, no matter how untalented, so far above the level of his normal achievement that he brings off dramatic effects beyond the reach of the most experienced actor in a spoken play. What has always so deeply disheartened me is that in opera these incomparable advantages of dramatic music have never been developed into a consistent, all-embracing style. The finest works contain things of the utmost nobility cheek by jowl with incomprehensible nonsense, expressionless conventionality and even downright frivolity.

Take that ugly juxtaposition you find nearly everywhere of absolute recitative and absolute aria ruling out all possibility of a true style, the whole musical flow being interrupted and impeded by this and by the faulty libretto on which it is based. In their finest scenes we do indeed find the great masters overcoming these evils by imparting a rhythmic-melodic significance to the recitative and by making it lead imperceptibly into the broader structure of a melody proper. This makes it all the more painful when suddenly we hear some banal chord announcing that once again dry recitative is about to be sung. And then, equally suddenly, in comes the full orchestra announcing the aria with its customary ritornello – that same ritornello which already in previous connecting passages the master had employed so expressively that its speaking eloquence threw a most interesting light on the dramatic situation. But what if such true blossoms of art are immediately followed by a number deliberately designed to cater for the lowest taste? – if a movingly beautiful and noble phrase is suddenly rounded off by the standard cadenza with its obligatory two runs and artificially prolonged last note, during which the singer unexpectedly turns his back upon the person he has been addressing and goes down to the footlights to give his claque the signal to applaud?

It is true that it is not really among the great masters that one finds these inconsistencies, but rather among the composers who sometimes surprise us by their capacity to rise to those heights I spoke of. What is so deplorable is that notwithstanding all the great masters' noble achievements, which have already brought operatic style near to perfection, these relapses keep on recurring – indeed, artificiality nowadays seems more prevalent than ever.

Undoubtedly the principal reason for this is the tendency of weaker artistic natures to allow themselves to be degraded by the character of the opera-going public. I have been told that Weber himself – that pure, deep, noble spirit – was sometimes afraid of carrying the dictates of style too far: he gave his wife what he called the right of the 'gallery' and allowed this 'gallery's' objections to persuade him here and there not to be too strict with his style and make a few discreet concessions.

These 'concessions', which Weber, my beloved first model, still felt compelled to make to the opera-going public – these 'concessions' you will not, I think I may justly claim, find in my *Tannhäuser*. And this is, perhaps, the essential difference between my opera and those of its predecessors. This called for no particular courage on my part – what I had observed of the public's reactions to the best in conventional opera led me to form a very high opinion indeed of its judgment. The artist whose work is intended to appeal not to abstract intellect, but to intuitive feeling, takes great and deliberate care to present it to the public and not just the connoisseur – his only reason for worry is the extent to which the critical approach may have caused the public to lose touch with its genuinely human reactions. In my view conventional opera has precisely this effect, thanks to those glaring concessions it contains; not knowing what to make of them, people get so confused that they cannot help passing hasty, false, judgments, and their confusion is further confounded by the chatter in their midst of those who call themselves experts. At a spoken play the public is much surer of itself: nothing in the world can convince an audience that an absurd plot makes sense, that an unsuitable speech is appropriate or a false accent true – all of which provides solid grounds for assuming that a self-confident and truly understanding public could be established for opera too.

Another respect in which *Tannhäuser* departs from opera in the accepted sense is the *dramatic poem* upon which it is based. I attach no value to the poem as a literary product, but I do assert that, even though its basis is a legendary miracle, the drama is consistently developed and that its design and execution contain no concession to the banal demands of an operatic libretto. My primary aim is to compel the public to focus its attention upon the dramatic action so closely that it is never for a moment lost sight of: all the musical elaboration must be experienced simply as the presentation of this action. From which it follows that it was my determination not to compromise the drama which enabled me to resist making any concessions to the musical treatment as well. Here indeed you have the clearest indication of what my so-called 'innovations' really consist of: it is anything but the tendency to be governed by absolute musical considerations of which people have taken upon themselves to accuse me with their 'Music of the Future'.

Finally I would like to say that, notwithstanding the great difficulty of producing a completely satisfactory translation of the text, it is with a sense of confidence that I am offering my *Tannhäuser* to the Parisian public. An enterprise which a few years ago would have been a source of great anxiety I now undertake less as an exercise in speculation than as a labour of love. That my feelings have so changed is primarily due to certain personal experiences during this latest stay of mine in Paris. Among them was one which particularly surprised and delighted me. You, my honoured friend, permitted me to approach you as a person to whom I was known and familiar. Though you had never attended a performance of my operas in Germany you had spent a considerable time carefully perusing my scores and had come, so you assured me, to like them. This had aroused in you the wish to see them performed here, and furthermore you were of the opinion that their performance in Paris would make a favourable and not insignificant impression. Since you thus gave me grounds for confidence you will, I hope, not reproach me for wearying you in return with this, perhaps, too comprehensive communication, and be willing to attribute the excessive zeal with which I have met your wish to my earnest desire to give the admirers of my work in this city a somewhat clearer view of my ideas. I would not want to put anyone to the trouble of seeking them for himself in my previous writings on the subject.

II
On Conducting

'... [Wagner's conducting] was described to me; the body, of no more than middle height, with its stiff deportment, the movement of the arms not immoderately great or sweeping, but decisive and very much to the point; showing no restlessness, in spite of his vivacity; usually not needing a score at a concert; fixing his expressive glance on the players and ruling the orchestra imperially, like the Weber he used to admire as a boy. The old flautist Fürstenau of Dresden told me often, when Wagner conducted one had no sense of being led. Each believed himself to be following freely his own feeling, yet they all worked together wonderfully. It was Wagner's mighty will that . . . had overborne their single wills, so that each thought himself free, while in reality he only followed the leader, whose artistic force lived and worked in him. "Everything went so easily and beautifully that it was the height of enjoyment", said Fürstenau; and the eyes of the old artist gleamed with joyful enthusiasm.'

Weingartner

TRANSLATOR'S NOTE

In one of the passages omitted in this abridged re-translation of *On Conducting* Wagner delivered a warning against the abuse of its fundamental doctrine – modification of tempo – which I take the opportunity of this Note to reproduce:

> 'Undoubtedly it is a valid objection that nothing could be more harmful than to introduce arbitrary changes of tempo that would throw open the door to the caprices of every conceited time-beater out to make an effect. . . .'

As on the rostrum Wagner exposed himself to the charge of arbitrariness, so in this essay. Many eyebrows will be raised, I should think, by his demand for a gently retarded delivery of the opening of the lively first variation of the second movement of the *Kreutzer* Sonata, in order to relate the opening to the mood of the andante theme (see p. 70): likewise by his demand that the repeated C flat quavers in the first bar of the development section of the slow movement of Mozart's G minor Symphony no. 40 should be delivered with a 'finely moulded crescendo' (see p. 84). Such glimpses of the way his genius for music drama acted upon his purely musical genius make the essay even more revelatory than he intended it to be.

MOTTO ADAPTED FROM GOETHE

'Fliegenschnauz' und Mückennas'
Mit euren Anverwandten,
Frosch im Laub und Grill' im Gras,
Ihr seid mir Musikanten!'

'Flies' snouts, gnats' noses,
Your friends and relations,
Tree-frogs, grass-crickets,
You are my musicians!'

ON CONDUCTING

Wagner was adapting the lines describing the musicians at Oberon and Titania's golden wedding in the *Walpurgisnacht* intermezzo of *Faust*. He gave them a polemical twist by converting the original last line, 'These are the musicians!' ('Das sind die Musikanten!') into 'You are my musicians!'

My purpose in the following pages is to record my experiences and observations in a field of musical activity hitherto practised merely as a routine, to which no standards of judgment are applied. In delivering my own judgments I shall be addressing myself not to conductors themselves but to instrumentalists and singers, since they are the ones who know whether they are being well or badly conducted – this knowledge in the nature of the case being one they can only account for when they are well conducted, which seldom happens. What I have in mind is not to impose a system but to record a number of observations to be extended as and when the context demands.

How their works are presented to the public is obviously a matter of importance to composers, since only a good performance can give the right impression and a bad one can make the music unrecognizable. The situation in the concert halls and opera houses of Germany can be understood by anyone willing and able to follow my account of the factors involved.

The glaring weaknesses of German orchestras are mainly due to the poor quality of conductors in their roles of Kapellmeister, Music Director and so forth. The choice and appointment of these people has been made with increasing carelessness as demands on the orchestra have become increasingly exacting. In the days when a Mozart score was the supreme test, the man in charge was the typical German Kapellmeister who was always in his own *locale* an important personage: reliable, strict, despotic and often rude. One of the last survivors of this breed I knew was Friedrich Schneider of Dessau; Guhr in Frankfurt was another. Their attitude to new music was typical of the old-style 'peruke' [Zöpfe] Kapellmeister; yet how effectively they could deal with it in their own way I myself experienced at a performance of *Lohengrin* in Karlsruhe under the old Kapellmeister Strauss. This most worthy man was obviously thrown into a state of concern, timidity and bewilderment by my score, but his concern led to a performance that could not have been stronger and more precise: everything was under control; he stood no nonsense; he held all his people in the hollow of his hand. Strange to say, this old gentleman is the only conductor I can think of who really had fire; though hurried, his tempos were always vital and well executed. I had a similar impression from H. Esser's performance of *Lohengrin* in Vienna.

What disqualified all those conductors of the old school – whether gifted like the above-mentioned or not – from dealing with the more complicated modern orchestral music was first and foremost the way they clung to the traditional method of orchestral seating. I cannot think of a single case anywhere in Germany of a fundamental re-arrangement being made to meet the demands of this music. In the big orchestras ancient rules still governed the promotion of players to front desks, so that by the time they reached them their powers had weakened, while behind them sat younger better players – in the case of the wind an especially unfortunate arrangement. And although in the recent past discerning efforts – not to mention the modest intelligence of the players themselves – have led to a reduction of these practices, there remains another involving string players whose damaging effects are still with us. Second violins and violas, especially the latter, are continually being victimized without any thought being given to the matter. Almost everywhere one finds violas played either by infirm violinists or else by worn-out wind players who at some stage took up the violin. A really good viola player is only called in when here or there a solo passage has to be dealt with – in my experience the first violin once had to lend a helping hand. And out of a large orchestra with eight viola players only one was capable of accurately performing the numerous difficult passages in one of my recent scores. Apart from considerations of charity this state of affairs was due to the fact that in earlier scores violas were mainly employed only to fill in the accompaniment; also the inferior orchestration of the Italian operas, which are still the mainstay of the repertoire, provided a justification. Since it is above all those Italian favourites that the big theatre intendants rely on (in accordance with the taste of the courts they serve, needless to say), it is not surprising that demands made by works frowned upon by those gentlemen could only have been met if the Kapellmeister carried weight and was convinced of their necessity. But most of our older Kapellmeisters were incapable of grasping the need for a fuller body of strings to counterbalance the greatly increased number of wind instruments. Even when the imbalance was glaringly obvious they did nothing to raise the celebrated German orchestras to the level of French ones whose violins, and their cellos, too, were far more powerful and efficient.

On Conducting

To make good these limitations of the old-style Kapellmeister should have been the object of the conductors of a later period. But intendants took good care to exclude anybody likely to assert himself as those earlier ones had done.

It will be worth while to consider how this later generation of conductors, who dominate music-making in Germany to-day, attained their position.

Since orchestras owe their maintenance to the various large and small court theatres – in short, to the theatre – it devolved upon theatre directors to select the conductors who, often for as long as half a century, would represent the spirit and dignity of German music. Presumably most of these conductors knew perfectly well how they came by this privilege; that merit had nothing to do with it (except in a very few cases) was obvious. They attained those so-called 'good positions' – that was the only light in which their patrons regarded them – through the simple operation of the law of inertia: they were pushed upwards. This, I believe, was how the great Berlin court orchestra acquired most of its conductors. True, sometimes things went by leaps and bounds: some new great man would suddenly appear under the protection of the lady-in-waiting of a princess or some such. The harm such people have done to our greatest orchestras and opera houses is beyond reckoning. They have only been able to maintain themselves by kowtowing to ignorant commonplace tolerant officials and pandering to the lazy habits of the musicians in their charge. By throwing discipline to the winds – not that they were ever capable of exercising it – and acceding to every demand from above, however senseless, these masters made themselves liked by all and sundry. Difficulties at rehearsals were got over by soothing references to the 'fame' of 'His Royal Highness's Chapel' made with smirks of mutual satisfaction. Who was there to notice that the standards of famous institutions declined from year to year? Where were the genuine masters who could judge them? Certainly not among the critics who only bark when they aren't muzzled and how to muzzle *them* is common knowledge.

In recent times, however, these positions have been occupied by persons specially qualified: according to the need or mood of the responsible authority an expert is brought in from somewhere or other in order to stir up the sluggish local Kapellmeister. These are the people who 'bring out' an opera in fourteen days, and understand very well how to 'make cuts' and how to write effective 'endings' into other people's scores. To this day skills such as these are exercised by one of the Dresden court chapel's oldest conductors.

Sometimes, though, persons of real distinction, really 'great' men, are sought after. They are not to be found in the theatre – but according to reports in the great political newspapers, conservatories and concert establishments turn them out every two or three years. These are the musical bankers of our day, trained in the school of Mendelssohn or recommended by him. A very different type, this, from the inept descendants of the old-style 'perukes' – musicians not reared in an orchestra or theatre but properly trained in newly founded conservatories, composing oratorios and psalms and attending the rehearsals of subscription concerts. They've been trained to conduct too and not only that: they are persons of breeding and education, which is more than can be said of their predecessors. There was no longer any question of rudeness. But neither were they afflicted by the diffidence of those poor native Kapellmeisters who had been chosen to replace the old-style despots: these gentlemen had *bon ton*, they knew how to behave, and the discomfort they inevitably felt in our 'peruke'-ridden German society made this knowledge all the more valuable. I do not doubt that these people have done some good to our orchestras: much that was crude and ridiculous has been abolished; details of elegant expression have been treated with more care. They were at home with the modern orchestra – indeed, thanks to their master Mendelssohn, the possibilities revealed by Weber's glorious genius have undergone a particularly delicate and refined development.

What these gentlemen primarily lacked was the energy to bring about the necessary reconstitution of our orchestras and of the institutions connected with them – the energy that goes with a self-confidence relying upon its own strength. Sad to say, everything about them – their reputation, talent and culture, even their faiths and loves and hopes – was artificial. Each was too taken up with his own affairs, too involved in the difficulties of his own position, to be capable of a broad general view of the situation as a whole and of the forces making for change. Having taken over from the old-style Kapellmeister because the latter had sunk so low that he could not understand the modern style and all that it involved, they appear to have felt themselves to be in a transition period: the German ideal of art, the goal of all noble endeavour, they did not know what to do about it because at bottom it was strange to them. In their hands the exacting demands of modern music were mere expedients. Meyerbeer, for example, was meticulous: in Paris he paid out of his own pocket for a good flautist to execute a certain passage. Since he understood very well the importance of a good performance, and apart from that was wealthy and independent, he could have done a very great deal for the Berlin orchestra when the King of Prussia appointed him 'Generalmusikdirektor'. Mendelssohn also was appointed and nobody can deny that he possessed the most extraordinary accomplishments and expertise. They were both hampered, of course, by the obstacles which have always stood in the way of progress there – but they of all people should have overcome them seeing how uniquely equipped they were. Why then did their strength fail them? Evidently because they hadn't really any strength. They let things slide – and the result is the 'famous' Berlin orchestra as we now see it, an orchestra from which the last trace of the Spontini tradition has disappeared. And this is Meyerbeer and Mendelssohn we are talking of! What can be expected from their elegant imitators who function in other places? – what indeed?

The lesson to be drawn from this survey of the successors of the old-style Kapellmeister and of the members of this latest breed is that not much is to be expected from them in the way of orchestral reform. In the past it was the instrumentalists who supplied the initiative, the reason of course being the increasing development of technical virtuosity. Undoubtedly this has been a benefit, but the benefit would have been still greater if conductors had played the part they should have done. Those successors of the older generation who had been pushed into their positions or owed them to the patronage of a lady-in-waiting or piano teacher were of course completely eclipsed by virtuosos: in the orchestra the latter played the role a prima donna does in the theatre. The elegant Kapellmeister of the new school, on the other hand, aligned himself with the virtuoso, which in some respects was all to the good, but could only have been a truly creative alliance if the spirit of German music had been truly understood by these gentlemen.

In this context it must be borne in mind that the opera was the main focus of their activities since orchestras owe their existence to the theatre. It was their business therefore to understand opera, to regard it not simply as music but as an art involving the application of drama to music, an application one might roughly compare to that of mathematics to astronomy. Had they understood this – and what I am referring to here is of course the application to music of dramatic song and expression – it would have illumined their conducting, especially of modern German music. In my case the clue to the right tempo and expression in Beethoven was provided years ago by the inspired delivery of the great Schröder-Devrient. Take that passage for solo oboe in the first movement of the C minor Symphony just after the beginning of the recapitulation:

Ex.1

I could no longer bear hearing that moving passage thrown away as it invariably was. Furthermore my handling of it made me realise the importance of the first violins' fermata in the corresponding passage of the exposition:

Ex.2

and the powerful impression I drew from those two apparently insignificant details led to a fresh understanding of the movement as a whole.... If only these conductors had the right attitude to the theatre how their conducting would have benefited! But they regard opera simply as tiresome drudgery (an attitude for which its sorry state in the German theatres provides a grim excuse) and seek their glory in the concert halls from which they were recruited. For, as I have said, whenever an intendant is seized by the desire to have a musician of reputation for Kapellmeister it is not in the theatre that he looks for him.

It comes to this, then, that before passing judgment on the achievements in the theatre of these one-time concert and conservatoire conductors we must visit them in the place where they built their reputation of solid German musicianship. We must study them in the concert hall.

When I was young, orchestral performances of the classics always left me feeling dissatisfied, and I still have that feeling whenever I attend them. What had seemed so full of life and soul played on the piano or read in the score I could hardly recognize. Above all I was astonished by the flabby delivery of Mozart's expressive cantilena. I discovered the reasons for this later (I expounded them in my *Report on a Music School in Munich*[1] which I recommend to those seriously interested). Certainly the principal reason is the lack of a truly German conservatory in the literal sense of the term, i.e. an institution in which the traditions of performance established by the masters themselves are conserved – which presupposes of course that from time to time the said masters should have actually performed their works there and demonstrated what they wanted. But unfortunately

---

[1] The *Report* was written in the spring of 1865, a year after Wagner's rescue by Ludwig.

German culture has missed all such opportunities; to-day in order to understand a classical piece we have to rely upon whatever idea this or that individual conductor may have of its tempo and expression.

In the days of my youth the famous concerts of the Leipzig *Gewandhaus* were not conducted at all: led by the first violin, Mathai, they were played through in the way that overtures and incidental music to dramas were. Regularly every winter, with nobody to wave a disturbing baton above him, Mathai led smooth precise performances of the principal works of the classical repertory, which in themselves present no great technical difficulties; the orchestra knew every note and one could see how gladly they welcomed the annual reappearance of those favourites.

The one work they couldn't manage was Beethoven's Ninth Symphony; nevertheless as a point of honour it too was played every year. I myself had made a copy of the score and worked out a piano arrangement for two hands. The utterly confusing impression given by the *Gewandhaus* performances astonished me, and eventually so discouraged me that I was thrown into doubt about Beethoven and for quite a while gave up studying him. It has also been very instructive to me that I only fully came to appreciate Mozart's instrumental works later when I myself had the opportunity to conduct them and give rein to my feeling for a truly expressive delivery of the Mozartian cantilena. The most instructive experience of all, though, was the performance I heard of the problematic 'Ninth' by the so-called Conservatoire Orchestra of Paris in 1839. The scales fell from my eyes; in a flash I divined the secret of its performance. In every bar the orchestra had been trained to perceive the Beethovenian *melody*, which our worthy Leipzig players had never noticed – and the orchestra *sang* that melody.

That was the secret. Not that the orchestra had been guided to it by a conductor of outstanding genius. Habeneck, the man responsible for the great merit of the performance, had spent a whole winter rehearsing the symphony and been left with an impression of unintelligibility and ineffectiveness. Whether a German conductor would have acknowledged such a feeling and left it at that is hard to say; Habeneck, at any rate, was moved to devote two more years to a study of the symphony and not to give up until the new Beethovenian *melos* had been understood and properly executed by his players, all of whom had a musicianly feeling for melodic expression. Habeneck, it must be understood, was a music director of the old style: he was the master and his word was law.

I still find it impossible to describe the beauty of that performance. To give an idea of it I will choose a passage from the first movement (I could have chosen many others) throwing light on the difficulty of interpreting Beethoven and the shortcomings of German orchestras:

I have never been able, not even with the best orchestras, to get this passage delivered with the perfect evenness of those musicians of the Paris Conservatoire heard thirty years ago. This single passage, remembered so often in my later life, brought home to me what is involved in orchestral interpretation because here tempo, legato and dynamics are bound up with each other. The ability of the Parisians to perform it exactly as written was the proof of their mastery. Neither in Dresden nor London nor anywhere else have I ever succeeded in getting the changes of bowing and strings in the repeated ascending figure made imperceptibly. It was equally impossible to have the whole passage played evenly without any accents since players always tend to get louder on ascending notes and softer on descending ones. Thus we always found ourselves making a *crescendo* in the fourth bar, with the inevitable consequence that the sustained G flat of the fifth bar was still more strongly accented, thereby completely ruining its effect in the context. Beethoven with his *sempre pp* clearly indicated what he wanted; the result of ignoring that expression-mark is hard to convey to the uninitiated; certainly the music is still expressing discontent, unrest, longing – but the *quality* of this expression can only be grasped when it is performed as the composer intended, as it was in Paris in 1839. I shall never forget the dynamic monotony (the reader must pardon this senseless description of a phenomenon impossible to put into words) of the unusual, even eccentric, intervals mounting to the tenderly sustained G flat, answered by a likewise sustained G natural. I shall never forget how I felt myself transported to a magic realm where all mysteries of the spirit are dissolved and everything made clear to understanding.

    I shall not pursue the spiritual aspect of that revelation; here my object is to consider in the light of practical experience what it was that enabled those Parisian musicians to perform this difficult passage so perfectly. In the first place it was obviously because they were conscientious painstaking musicians, not content to soothe each other with mutual compliments, not presuming to know everything already but capable of humility when faced with something unintelligible and endeavouring to get their bearings by applying to it the implement they were at home with, namely their technique. French musicians are trained in the Italian school and the result, in itself excellent, of the Italian influence is that they can only grasp music as song: in their eyes playing an instrument well means making it sing. So, as I have said, that splendid orchestra *sang* this symphony. But if it was to be sung correctly then the *right tempo* would have had to be found throughout – which brings me to the other aspect of the matter that impressed itself upon me. Old Habeneck was not guided by any abstract aesthetic inspiration; he had no 'genius'. *He found the right tempo because he took infinite pains to get his orchestra to understand the* melos *of the symphony.*

Only a correct understanding of the melos *sets the right tempo;* the two are indivisible, the one conditions the other. I do not hesitate to condemn as inadequate the great majority of our performances of the classical instrumental works because I am convinced that *our conductors cannot set the right tempo since they know nothing about singing.* I have never met a German Kapellmeister or any other kind of music director really able to sing a melody, whether his voice is good or bad. For in the eyes of all of them music is an abstract thing apart, a cross between grammar, arithmetic and gymnastics – which of course explains why the initiated are only fit to teach in a conservatory or some other kind of musical gymnasium. One cannot imagine them breathing life and soul into an actual performance.

In what follows I shall pursue this topic in the light of a discussion of my own experiences.

What decides whether a conductor is performing a work correctly is his choice of tempo: if the choice is right we know at once whether he has understood the work. The right tempo enables good players as they get to know a piece to find the fitting expression almost of their own accord, since the conductor's choice of tempo will have been conditioned by his understanding of the expression. That choice of his, however, is obviously no easy matter since it is only from an understanding of the correct expression in every regard that the right tempo can be found.

It is for this reason that Haydn, Mozart and the other masters as a rule instinctively confined themselves to tempo indications of the most general kind: 'Andante', 'Allegro' and 'Adagio' with various simple degrees of 'more' or 'less' was all they thought necessary. Bach hardly ever gave any tempo indication at all, and in a purely musical sense this is the ideal course. It is as though he were asking 'how can one who does not understand my themes and figures and feel their character and expression be helped by an Italian tempo indication?' My own experience bears this out. I supplied my early operas with lavish tempo indications and employed a metronome in order to exclude (so I supposed) any possibility of mistake. The result was that when I had cause to complain of a stupid tempo in, for example, *Tannhäuser*, the defence was invariably made that my metronome-mark had been scrupulously observed. This brought home how unsafe it was to apply mathematics to music. I never used the metronome again. Instead I only gave very general indications of the main tempo, paying particular attention to its modifications, a matter about which our conductors know next to nothing. I have since been told that those indications of mine because they are so general have upset and confused conductors, and all the more so because they were expressed in German: accustomed as they are to the conventional Italian terms they found it hard to understand what I meant by, for example, 'Mässig' [Moderate]. This complaint was made to me recently by a conductor whom I have to thank for performing my *Rhinegold* in no less than three hours according to a report in the Augsburg *Allgemeine Zeitung;* whereas when it was rehearsed by a conductor under my supervision it took only two and a half.[2] A similar report was once made to me about a performance of *Tannhäuser:* what sort of performance it was could be gathered from the fact that the overture which I conducted in Dresden in twelve minutes took twenty. We are dealing here of course with hopeless dunderheads whom the very sight of an Alla Breve beat terrifies: they have to cling to the normal four-in-a-bar in order to reassure themselves that they really are conducting and making themselves felt. How these donkeys from our village churches ever found their way into our orchestras God alone knows!

Dragging, on the other hand, is definitely *not* the feature that stamps the elegant conductors of recent times: their fatal tendency is to hurry. Thereby hangs a tale worth telling for the light it throws on the generally accepted style of current music-making.

Robert Schumann once complained to me that in the Leipzig concerts Mendelssohn had spoilt all his pleasure in the Ninth Symphony by taking the first movement too fast. The only time I myself heard Mendelssohn conducting a Beethoven symphony was at a rehearsal of the Eighth in Berlin. I noticed how – almost capriciously, so it seemed – he would pick out a detail here and there and work away at it so determinedly and with such excellent results that I was left wondering why he hadn't devoted the same attention to other details. Even so, under him this incomparably gay symphony flowed extraordinarily smoothly and pleasantly. More than once in conversation he remarked that a too slow tempo was very damaging and that he always gave the advice that it was better to take a piece too

---

[2] The conductor under Wagner's supervision was Hans Richter (1843-1916); the other was the Munich court Kapellmeister Franz Wüllner (1832-1902).

fast; a really good performance, after all, was always a rarity, but one could give the impression of one if the music were played in such a way that not too much was noticed and this could best be done by covering the ground quickly. Mendelssohn's pupils must have heard him expressing these views at greater length and in more detail – certainly those remarks of his were not merely intended for my ear: I had plenty of opportunity to realise this later when I perceived the effects of such maxims and came to understand the reasons for them.

One such opportunity was my experience with the orchestra of the London Philharmonic Society which Mendelssohn had often conducted. There his methods had imprinted themselves as established traditions – though one could easily have thought that it was the concerts themselves that had established the methods, so admirably suited were they to the Londoners' customs and peculiarities. Since an enormous amount of instrumental music was played and only one rehearsal allowed for each performance, I often had to leave the orchestra to its traditions and in so doing was often reminded of what Mendelssohn had said to me. The music flowed like water out of a fountain; to hold back was unthinkable; every allegro finished as a presto. To interfere was troublesome and embarrassing since the proper well-controlled tempo exposed the defects hidden beneath the flow. The orchestra played everything *mezzoforte*; a genuine *forte*, a genuine *piano* was never heard. So far as possible I did eventually manage in important passages to impose my idea of the correct expression and corresponding tempo. The players themselves did not object, indeed were only too pleased, and the public demonstrated its approval. Only the critics raged – indeed so furiously that at the request of the intimidated committee of the Society I let the orchestra scamper through the slow movement of Mozart's E flat major Symphony, no. 39 in their habitual way as Mendelssohn himself had done.

Eventually I had the experience of hearing that fatal maxim actually voiced by a professor of counterpoint, Mr Potter (if I remember rightly), a very amiable elderly gentleman whose symphony I had to perform.[3] He begged me to play the Andante rather fast because he was afraid it might bore the audience. I pointed out that however fast one played the audience was sure to be bored if the performance was limp and expressionless, whereas it wouldn't be if his simple pretty theme were performed as he had sung it to me – that surely was what he had wanted. Mr Potter was obviously touched; he admitted I was right and excused himself on the ground that he had ceased to consider the possibility of that kind of

---

[3] Cipriani Potter (1792-1871) was principal of the R.A.M. from 1835 to 1859. He was not a 'professor of counterpoint' but a notable pianist, piano-teacher, composer and conductor.

performance. The symphony was played that evening and after the Andante he joyfully pressed my hand.

The lack of feeling for proper tempo and expression among musicians today, even the foremost ones, is indeed astonishing. Thus I found it impossible to get Mendelssohn to share my view that the rhythm generally adopted for the third movement of Beethoven's Eight Symphony is exasperatingly wrong. Here we have another example worth considering for the light it throws upon a matter of serious import.

It is well known that in his later important symphonies Haydn quickened the tempo of his minuet-and-trio movements, thereby converting them into a refreshing transition between his adagios and finales. In the trios especially he incorporated the *Ländler* of the period, so that the term *Menuetto* no longer applied to the tempo and became merely traditional. Even so, in my opinion Haydn's minuets are usually taken too fast. Certainly Mozart's are. I have in mind the Minuet of the G minor Symphony, no. 40, and still more so that of the C major, no. 41. If the orchestra gambol through the latter as though it were a presto then the important dotted minims of the Trio go for nothing:

Ex.4

What is needed here is a steady, cheerful, festal gait.

The Minuet of the Eighth Symphony, however, Beethoven conceived in a traditional sense, as he did sometimes in other works. Together with the preceding *Allegretto scherzando* it formed a contrast with the two allegro outer movements, and so, in order to make his intention clear he marked it not merely *Menuetto* but *Tempo di Menuetto*. The novelty of these two middle movements is nearly always overlooked: the *Allegretto scherzando* is treated as though it were the usual Andante and the *Tempo di Menuetto* as though it were the usual Scherzo, and since neither accordingly makes its proper effect this marvellous symphony is generally regarded by musicians as a side-product of Beethoven's muse, a relaxation after the tremendous effort of the Seventh Symphony. After having dragged the *Allegretto scherzando* one does one's level best to make an invigorating *Ländler* out of the *Tempo di Menuetto* with the result that at the end we simply don't know what we have been listening to. One is only too thankful when the martyrdom of the Trio is over: the cellos' accompanying triplets taken at a fast tempo:

Ex.5

convert that most delightful of idylls into a veritable monstrosity. The passage is notoriously difficult for cellists because it is impossible to avoid a painful effect of scratching when those staccato triplets are taken fast. The difficulty solves itself when the tempo matches the tender lyricism of the horn and clarinet melodies; also things are made easier for the clarinettist: he is spared the anxiety even the finest players feel of emitting a 'quack'. I remember the orchestra's sigh of relief when, taken at the proper moderate tempo, the basses' and bassoons' humorous *sforzandi* in the penultimate bars made their proper effect:

Ex.6
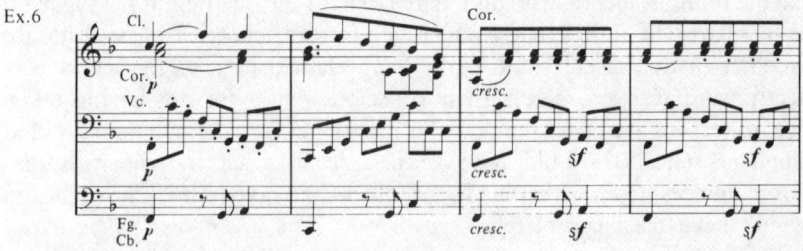

The short *crescendo*s became distinct, the tender *pianissimo* of the ending made its effect, and the main part of the movement acquired the comfortable weighty expression it ought to have:

Ex.7

I once attended in the company of Mendelssohn a performance of this symphony in Dresden conducted by the late Kapellmeister Reissiger; I raised the above-mentioned problem of tempo, telling him that Reissiger (who was my colleague at that time) had accepted my solution – so at any rate I had assumed since he had promised to take the movement more slowly. We listened. The third movement began and I was shocked to hear the same old *Ländler* tempo again. Before I could make any comment Mendelssohn turned to me with an approving nod and smile saying 'Yes, that's right! Bravo!' My shock gave way to astonishment. For a reason I shall give below I was not inclined to blame Reissiger all that much. But Mendelssohn's insensitivity raised doubts as to whether he had really noticed what had happened. I seemed to be staring into a veritable abyss of superficiality, a complete emptiness.

The third movement of the Eighth Symphony was treated in exactly the same fashion shortly afterwards by a conductor of repute, one of Mendelssohn's successors as director of the Leipzig concerts.[4] As Reissiger had done, he agreed with my view of the right tempo and promised to observe it at a forthcoming concert to which he invited me. The reason he gave for breaking his word was an odd one: he laughingly pleaded forgetfulness. He had been so distracted by various directorial responsibilities that it was only after the movement had begun that he recalled his promise; obviously he couldn't suddenly change the familiar tempo he'd already set, and so on that occasion had had to let things take their course. Annoyed though I was, I at least had the satisfaction of having found someone who understood what I meant and did not regard it as a matter of indifference which tempo one chose. Indeed I doubt whether in this case I could really have blamed him, for he had a perfectly valid reason – albeit an unconscious one – for not having taken the movement at a faster tempo. To alter in performance a tempo decided upon at rehearsal would have been a reckless act fraught with dire consequences, from which his forgetfulness had saved him. The orchestra would have been completely thrown out, *since a different tempo would have inevitably meant a completely different style of performance.*

Here we reach the decisive point that must be clearly grasped before we can understand why performances of our classics are so careless and ridden with bad habits. A bad habit, in that it is bound up with the tempo, has a certain justification: it gives a performance a degree of uniformity; for though the root of the evil is concealed, the effect would obviously be still worse if *only* the tempo of a habitual style of performance were suddenly altered.

To make this clear I shall choose the simplest possible example: the opening of the C minor Symphony:

Ex.8

---

[4] Ferdinand Hiller (1811-1885).

Our conductors usually make light of that fermata, dwelling on it only in order to keep the orchestra on its toes for a precise delivery of the figure in the next two bars. The time they spend on the E flat is the time normally taken by a violinist's bow to sustain a *forte*. But now suppose Beethoven's voice were heard from the grave calling to our conductors:

'Hold that fermata of mine! Cling to it! I was not making a joke; I was not waiting to decide what to do next. I was pouring out the heartfelt emotion of my adagios and hurling it into the stormy figuration of this violent movement in order to grip you with terror and rapture. Hold that E flat, therefore, as though you were wringing the last drop of life out of it. I was dividing the seas in order to behold the abyss beneath. I was parting the clouds in order to behold the shining sun and the blue sky. Therefore I put fermatas into this movement. You have only to look at the clear thematic intention of that sustained E flat after three short stormy notes and you will understand what the other ones are meant to convey.'

But if a conductor were to heed these words and get his strings to play accordingly what success would he have? Very little. The sustaining of the fermata would cause their bows to lose their initial impact, the tone would become ever thinner, it would dwindle to an embarrassed *piano*. This would happen – and here we are seeing one of the evil consequences of the present-day conductor's habits – because nothing has become so strange to our orchestras as *sustaining a note at an even level of strength*. Let every conductor demand an evenly sustained *forte* from no matter which instrument and he will find how unaccustomed the demand is and how much patient practising is needed to satisfy it.

And yet as in singing so with the orchestra: full, evenly sustained tone is the basis of all dynamics; only then is it possible to make the manifold nuances which stamp the character of a performance. Without that basis an orchestra has no strength – it can only make sounds. Conductors take no cognisance of this failing, since all they care about are the effects of an exaggerated *pianissimo*. For the strings this is easy, but it is very difficult for the wind, especially the woodwind. Indeed it is hardly possible for flautists to sustain a delicate *piano* now that the former gentle instrument has been converted into a powerful tube – French oboists, who have preserved the pastoral character of the instrument, and the clarinettist's 'echo effect' are the exceptions. This state of affairs, existing in our very best orchestras, raises the question: if the wind are incapable of producing an equivalent *piano* then why not restore the balance by having the strings play with a fuller tone instead of with that exaggerated softness which makes a positively ridiculous contrast? But obviously conductors are completely unaware of any imbalance. Regarded from another point of view, the cause of the trouble is the way string players produce their *piano:* as they are incapable of a proper *forte* so they are of a proper *piano*. Here again they have something to learn from wind players: it is all too easy to produce a whispering rustle by drawing the bow loosely across the strings; a wind player on the other hand needs a high degree of breath-control to sustain a quiet soft tone perfectly in tune. Violinists should study the full-bodied *piano* of first-rate wind players – and the latter for their part emulate the full bodied *cantabile* of the finest singers.

The extremes of softness and loudness are the twin poles of orchestral dynamics: what sort of performance do we get if neither the one nor the other is properly cultivated? How can dynamics be modified if those extremes aren't clearly indicated? Obviously such a performance must be so inadequate that that above-mentioned recommendation of Mendelssohn to cover the ground quickly is very useful – no wonder this maxim has been raised by our conductors to a veritable dogma, so much so that any attempt to rectify the performance of our classics is regarded by them as downright heresy.

Reverting to these conductors I must dwell yet again on the subject of tempo, the touchstone of the quality of a performance.

Obviously it is the character of a performance which determines the right tempo of a piece. The decisive factor is whether sustained tone (song) or rhythmic motion (figuration) should predominate. When he has made up his mind about this the conductor will know what kind of tempo to employ.

Here adagio stands to allegro as sustained tone does to figured motion. The time-signature 'Adagio' makes sustained tone the lawgiver: rhythm is dissolved in the self-sufficient flow of pure tone. In a certain subtle sense one could say of an adagio that it can never be taken slowly enough. When the power of the language of pure tone is given full play *languor* of feeling becomes an ecstasy. What in the allegro is expressed by changes of figuration is now expressed by the infinite variety of inflected tone – the slightest shift of harmony surprises, and by continually working on our feelings the remotest key change is anticipated.

None of our conductors pay sufficient heed to this; when they turn to an adagio their first step is to single out some piece of figuration and adjust their tempo to its presumed speed. Perhaps I am the only conductor who dares to take the third movement of the Ninth Symphony, marked *Adagio molto e cantabile*, at the truly adagio tempo its character demands. The alternation of this tempo with the *Andante moderato* of the section in triple time has the effect of drawing attention to its adagio quality – but this doesn't prevent conductors from blurring the contrast between the two until nothing is left but the change from common to triple time. The latter part of the movement in which the original 3/4 tempo becomes a 12/8 provides an instructive example of a pure adagio broken up by ornamental figuration:

Ex.9

The broad cantilena of the repeated original melody is now, as it were, the fixed image of the original – the *fixed* image because, whereas formerly the tempo could delicately fluctuate in order to allow free play for expressive tonal inflections, now the swift motion of ornamental figuration imposes the necessity of a uniform tempo. It remains to add that it is this necessity, when we study its consequences, which will provide us with the rule for handling the rhythm of an allegro.

Since sustained inflected tone is the basis of all truly musical performance we may take it that the adagio in the form developed by Beethoven in the slow movement of the Ninth Symphony is the basis of all truly musical rhythm. Indeed in a subtle sense the allegro can be regarded as the consequence, carried to its furthest extreme, of rhythmic figuration breaking up the character of the adagio. And in the allegro itself, when we consider its principal motives more closely, we always find a predominant lyrical element derived from the adagio. Most of Beethoven's important allegro movements are founded upon a basic melody – hence the 'sentimental'[5] significance which distinguishes them so sharply from the earlier 'naive'[5] examples of the *genre*. Not that the difference is all that great between Beethoven's:

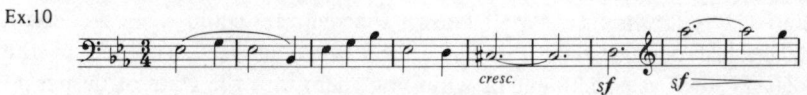

Ex.10

and Mozart's:

Ex.11

---

[5] Wagner explains his use of these terms on p. 66 below.

or:

Ex.12

With Mozart, as with Beethoven, the exclusively allegro character is felt when figuration has the upper hand; in other words, when the reaction of rhythmic motion against sustained tone is given its head. This is what usually happens in Rondo-finales; those of Mozart's no. 39 and Beethoven's Seventh are eloquent examples. Here rhythmic motion as such is celebrating its orgies and so these movements must be played with the utmost speed and tautness. What lies between these two extremes must be governed by a principle rooted in a sense of their *inter-relationship*, a principle which must be grasped in all its subtlety and manifold variety, since at bottom it is the same as that which governs the infinite variety of inflected tone. When I now turn to consider more closely this principle, summed up in the phrase, *modification of tempo* – a thing our conductors are so ignorant of that they stupidly denounce it as a heresy – the reader who has followed me thus far will realise that what we are dealing with is the principle conditioning the very life of music.

I have drawn a distinction above between two kinds of allegro: a later typically Beethovenian kind which I described as 'sentimental' and an earlier 'naive' kind associated chiefly with Mozart. In employing those terms I had in mind Schiller's eloquent characterization in his famous essay *On Naive and Sentimental Poetry*.[6]

It is not my purpose to enter into the aesthetic problem Schiller was dealing with: here it will suffice to point out that in applying the term 'naive' to Mozart's allegros I had in mind the fast *Alla Breve* ones. The most perfect examples are the operatic overtures, above all those to *Figaro* and *Don Giovanni*. It is well known that Mozart could never get them taken fast enough – at Prague, after having at last succeeded to the players' own astonishment in whipping them into the state of desperate courage needed to play the *Figaro* Overture presto, he exclaimed 'Well done! But on the evening faster still . . . !' He was quite right, of course. As in an ideal sense the pure adagio (as I have said) cannot be taken too slowly, so the pure allegro of that overture cannot be taken too fast. As ideally there are no limits to expressive tonal inflection, so there are none to the motion of rhythmic figuration. The boundary of what can actually be achieved is set by the laws of aesthetic balance: the extremes of

---

[6] Schiller employed the terms in order to draw a general distinction between the selfconscious emotionalism of contemporary writing and the unselfconscious poise of the ancient Greeks, and a particular one between his own turbulent dramas and the tranquil classicism of the later Goethe.

inhibited slow movement and uninhibited fast movement must be so handled that a resumption of the one or the other is experienced as an imperative necessity. Thus the sequence of movements in the symphonies of the classical masters – the Allegro; the Adagio; the intermediate Minuet or Scherzo in strict dance form; the extremely fast Finale – answers a deep need. It is a symptom of their failure to recognise this that composers today endeavour to eke out their boring ideas by reverting to the old-style Suite with its arbitrary stringing together of dance pieces – as though the Suite had not long ago given rise to a wealth of miscellaneous forms treated with far greater variety.

What stamps those absolute allegros of Mozart as 'naive' is their straightforward alternation of *forte* and *piano* passages, and furthermore their indiscriminate juxtaposition of stereotyped melodic-rhythmic formulae, which the master delivers either *piano* or *forte* with an indifference that is more than surprising (the same is true of his perpetually recurring bustling half-closes). But all this – not to mention the employment of utterly banal periods and phrases – is explained by the character of these allegros: cantilena plays no part; the perpetual restless motion is intended to induce a kind of intoxication. It is deeply significant that the *Don Giovanni* Overture at its close veers unmistakably into the realm of the 'sentimental'; its *molto allegro* having reached its 'boundary', as I termed it, the tempo has to be modified to that of the opening scene of the opera which, though still an Alla Breve, is not so fast. The change of tempo though vital must be unnoticeable:

Ex.13

Ex.14

That the majority of our conductors crudely ignore this feature of the *Don Giovanni* Overture is a matter I shall not dwell upon; what is important here is to emphasize that the character of this older 'naive' allegro is poles apart from the later 'sentimental' one typical of Beethoven. Mozart first learnt from the Mannheim orchestra what had hitherto been regarded as the novelty of *crescendo* and *diminuendo* in orchestral performances (the fact that expressive feeling had previously played no role in the management of the *piano* and *forte* sections of an allegro is also evident in the old masters' scoring).

How does the Beethovenian allegro relate to all this? What would happen if the *Eroica* Symphony (to take the most striking example of the changes he brought about) were taken at the strict tempo of Mozart's allegro overtures? Yet does it ever enter the heads of our conductors *not* to play it as they do those overtures, namely, straight through at a single tempo from the first bar to the last? In so far as one can talk here of a 'conception', the conductor – assuming he belongs to the fashionable school justifying himself with the Mendelssohnian *chi va presto, va sano* – leaves it to this or that member of the orchestra with a feeling for effect to make what he can of:

Ex.15

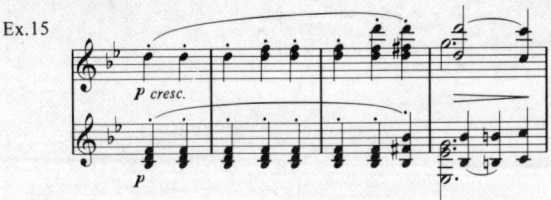

or of the wailful:

Ex.16

Such things are not the conductor's concern for he is on 'classical' ground, where everything is taken in one fell swoop, where 'grande vitesse', elegantly insistent, is the order of the day, where 'time is money'.

We have in fact at last reached the position from which a definitive judgment upon the whole world of present-day music-making can be delivered – as the reader will have noticed, to reach it I had to enter into a considerable amount of detail. I had to set forth the dilemma itself and make everybody feel that Beethoven introduced an entirely fresh element. What was previously insulated in closed forms is now – at least so far as the main motives are concerned – welded into a single all-encompassing form, in which the motives are presented together and the contrasts they generate are developed. This of course must be reflected in performance – above all the tempo must be handled with a delicacy matching the delicacy of the web of motives, which in the nature of the case declare their character through their motion.

At this point we must recognise that the application of the above-defined principle, *modification of tempo*, presents difficulties which are part and parcel of the whole difficulty of understanding these latest manifestations of the German genius. In the preceding pages I concentrated upon one of the brightest luminaries in the musical world in order to avoid the chaotic detail in which an account of my experiences with lesser figures would have entangled me. If now I do not hesitate to declare that the Beethoven whom public performances have hitherto presented is still a chimaera, I owe it to myself to justify this not undogmatic assertion by changing my stance: instead of dealing only with negative aspects I must adopt a positive standpoint and indicate how in my opinion Beethoven and those akin to him *should* be performed.

Since here too I face an inexhaustible wealth of detail I shall confine myself to a few striking examples of my experience.

One of the principal forms in music is the set of variations upon a given theme. Haydn, and after him Beethoven, converted its loose succession of dissimilar pieces into works of real artistic substance and this they achieved, apart from the wealth of their invention, by *relating dissimilarities to each other*. They did this most effectively by development: a rhythmic figure previously hinted at was carried further; a satisfying sense of surprise was created when something lacking in one variation was made good in the succeeding one. By such means the intrinsic structural weakness of a form that consisted of sharply contrasted pieces arbitrarily juxtaposed was concealed. Indeed it was precisely this weakness that Beethoven knew how to turn to account, avoiding any suggestion of the arbitrary or accidental; he did this at what I have termed the boundaries of sustained tone and fast movement: suddenly he evokes an overwhelming longing for contrast which he satisfies by making the one kind of motion follow upon the other. It is in his great works that he does this: one of the most instructive examples is the Finale of the *Eroica*, once we realise that in essence it is an immensely expanded set of variations and must therefore be interpreted with the utmost possible variety. This can only be done – and this is also true of other such movements – if the performer is aware of the above-mentioned weaknesses of the variation form and hence in a position to counteract them. Far too many variations consist of individual pieces arbitrarily aligned by convention. Worst of all is the effect of a peaceful theme followed by an incomprehensibly gay first variation. Thus the glorious andante theme of the variations of the *Kreutzer* Sonata:

Ex.17

is followed by a variation which has always struck me as a mere gymnastic exercise:

Ex.18

On Conducting

That is how every virtuoso treats it, upsetting me so much that I never want to hear any more of the movement. Curiously enough when I complain the reaction is invariably the same as when I object to the tempo of the Minuet-and-Trio movement of the Eighth Symphony. People agree 'on the whole', but have no idea what I am driving at.

Reverting to the *Kreutzer* Sonata – there is no denying that that first variation of the gloriously drawn-out andante theme is extraordinarily lively; Beethoven could hardly have conceived it as a piece that must immediately follow the theme because it was closely related to it; he must have been unconsciously influenced by the sectional structure of the variation form. In other movements of his, modelled on the variation form but conceived as continuous wholes (for example, the slow movements of the Fifth Symphony and of the great E flat Quartet, Op. 127, above all the second movement of the great C minor Sonata, Op.111) we admire the expressive refinement of the way the variations lead into each other. In a case such as that of the *Kreutzer* Sonata the performers might well claim to be acting as the master's representatives if they were to seek to relate the entry, at least, of the first variation to the mood of the theme by a certain restraint of tempo, which would have the effect of gently hinting at the new mood, instead of immediately establishing it as in all the performances one hears. If this were done with genuine artistry the variation would *gradually* become more lively; one would be gently eased out of the mood of the theme, and this would give the passage an additional charm.

A more striking example of a passage of this kind is provided by the C sharp Quartet, Op.131: I refer to the entry of the *Allegro molto vivace* after the opening *Adagio*:

Ex. 19

Ex. 19 continued

The tempo indication *Allegro molto vivace* applies to the new movement as a whole. Now one of the distinguishing features of this quartet is that not only is there no break between the movements but they are subtly developed out of each other. The opening *Adagio* conveys a mood of melancholy dreaming, unlike anything else in Beethoven; with the entry of the *Allegro molto vivace* it is as though a pleasant memory had suddenly come to mind and been seized and dwelt upon with growing excitement. Everything depends here on whether the change of heart after the numb, grief-laden *Adagio ma non troppo e molto espressivo* is effected in such a way that the suddenness of it does not jar. The new theme declares itself in a prolonged *pianissimo* as though it were the image of a dream faintly recognized – at the eighth bar it loses itself in a *ritardando* – then a *crescendo* and livelier tempo establishes its reality. Here it is the performer's plain duty to subtly modify the tempo of that *pianissimo* declaration. After the *Adagio's* closing:

Ex. 20

the changed tempo of the ensuing

must not be noticeable; only at the *crescendo* after the *ritardando*, only at the *crescendo* whose rhythmic significance is indicated by the master's expression-mark *in tempo*, should the faster rhythm take hold. Needless to say these modifications are never made: at every performance of this quartet the players throw themselves into the *molto vivace* as though it were an impudent joke and from now on all is fun and games. The effect is dreadful to anyone with a sense of artistic propriety. Yet people call this 'classical'!

Taking these examples as my cue, in what follows I shall consider more closely the demands of a correct performance of the classics. So doing, I shall run the risk of wounding distinguished musicians and Kapellmeisters with some unpleasant home-truths.

In setting forth the problems of tempo modification created by the later German classical music I have, I hope, sufficiently indicated the difficulties involved, difficulties which only discerning minds are capable of appreciating and solving. The Beethovenian 'sentimental' *genre* contains a variety of pre-existing 'naive' elements which the master makes rich use of: legato and staccato, cantilena and figuration are no longer insulated in separate forms, variations are no longer piled up as a mere series but subtly connected. There can be no doubt (as I have already amply demonstrated in certain cases) that if a suitable tempo is not found for a symphonic movement created out of such variegated elements the effect will be monstrous in the deepest, most literal sense. I remember how in my youth older musicians used to shake their heads over the *Eroica*. In Prague Dionys Weber handled it as though it actually were a monster. And no wonder: the Mozartian allegro being the only kind he understood, his pupils at the conservatory were made to perform the first movement in strict tempo and whoever heard them thought Dionys quite right. That movement has never been performed in any other way – and yet today the *Eroica* is universally acclaimed! But this is not just something to laugh at; there is a good reason for it, namely, that over the decades the symphony has been studied at the piano and in one way or another exercised its irresistible power there. Had that salvation not been possible and the symphony been left to the tender mercies of our Kapellmeisters etc, this noblest music of ours would never have survived.

These challenging views I shall now proceed to justify by citing a work whose popularity in Germany is second to none: the Overture to Weber's opera *Der Freischütz*.

How often has that overture been played! And yet only on one occasion have I met persons horrified to think how often they have heard this superb tone poem mangled and trivialized without their having realised it at the time. Those persons attended a concert I gave in Vienna in 1864 at which among other works I conducted this overture. At rehearsals the Vienna court opera orchestra, unquestionably one of the finest in the world, was completely put out by my demands. The introductory *Adagio*:

Ex. 22

was taken at the comfortable andante appropriate to the *Alphorn*[7] or some such pleasant composition. That this was not merely a Viennese tradition but common practice I had already discovered in Dresden, where Weber himself had conducted the work. When eighteen years after the master's death I myself conducted it there in my way, ignoring the habits permitted by my senior colleague, Reissiger, the elderly cellist, Dotzauer, who had played under Weber, turned to me saying earnestly: 'Yes, that was how Weber took it; this is the first time I've heard it done properly again.' Weber's widow was still living in Dresden, and the proofs I gave of my feeling for her husband's music led to her expressing the fervent wish that I would stay on a long time in my post of Kapellmeister: having abandoned all hopes, at last she was hearing his music performed as it should be. I mention this beautiful, precious tribute because the recollection of it has always fortified me against judgments of a different kind passed upon my conducting. Thus it emboldened me to make a clean sweep of the Vienna court orchestra's way of performing the *Freischütz* Overture. I made them re-study the hackneyed piece. Cheerfully following the lead of the gifted R. Lewi, the horns adjusted their instruments and converted the introduction, hitherto treated as a pompous show-piece, into a quiet forest phantasy, their melody and the strings' *pianissimo* accompaniment creating the magical effect Weber intended:

---

[7] A popular song of the day.

Ex. 23

Except at the required *mf* of bar 10 the horns sustained the hush of their *pianissimo*, giving only a gentle inflection instead of the customary *sforzando* to the accent in the penultimate bar before the melody dies away. In the succeeding bars:

Ex.24

the cellos converted their usual violent emphasis on the E flat above the strings' *tremolando* into the intended gentle sigh, so that now the ensuing terrifying *fortissimo* made its proper overwhelming effect. Having thus restored the mysterious sinister atmosphere at the close of the introduction, I gave free rein to the headlong rush of the turbulent allegro – I did this regardless of the lyrical second theme because I knew that when I reached it I would be able imperceptibly to *modify the tempo to one that would suit it.*

It goes without saying that it is precisely this incorporation of an adagio-like lyrical theme that fundamentally distinguishes this later type of variegated allegro movement from the earlier one. A perfect example is the second main theme of the *Oberon* Overture:

Ex. 25

whose character is far removed from that of an allegro proper. Technically of course it is the composer's purpose to weave such a theme into the main body of the movement: his whole tendency is towards unification. On the face of it therefore a lyrical theme lies entirely within the scheme of this kind of allegro. But if such a theme is to be brought to life the question arises: how should the tempo be modified so as to do justice both to the allegro's lyrical and other than lyrical aspects?

I must now resume my account of that performance I gave of the *Freischütz* Overture with the Vienna court theatre orchestra.

When after having worked the tempo up to fever heat I reached the long-drawn-out, adagio-like clarinet phrase:

Ex. 26
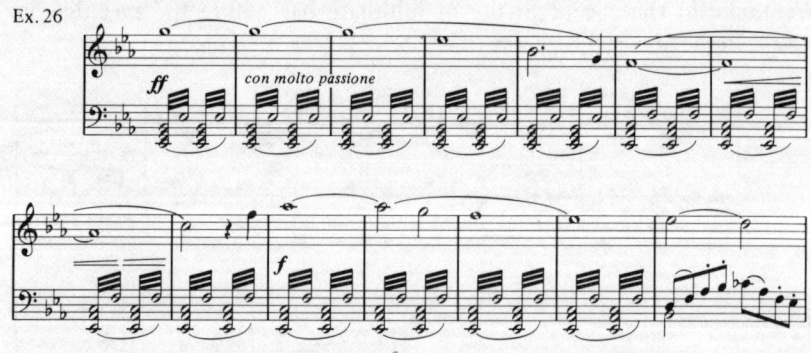

I took the opportunity to slow down imperceptibly the succeeding passage:

Ex. 27

Despite the animated:

this imperceptibly slower tempo led beautifully into the E flat *cantabile* theme and made it possible to deliver it with only the slightest modification of the main tempo of the movement:

Ex.29

I insisted on an even *piano* without the usual vulgarly accented *crescendo* and no breaks in the phrasing:

Ex.30

All this of course had to be explained to the excellent players. The effect was so strikingly successful that when we reached the passage after the *cantabile* they needed only the slightest hint to speed up imperceptibly the pulsating:

Ex.31

Ex.31 continued

At the ensuing *fortissimo*:

Ex.32

they responded enthusiastically to my demand for an emphatic reaffirmation of the main tempo. When the conflict between the sharply contrasted motives is compressed into shorter periods and worked out in a more urgent form, until eventually the desperate energy of the music lashes itself to a climax:

Ex.33

it was not so easy to do justice to the turmoil without upsetting the main tempo. It was especially here that continuous modification proved its value.

The orchestra was again surprised when in the final section, after the sustained *fortissimo* of the tremendous C major triad followed by a general pause:

Ex.34

I broke with custom by playing the – now jubilant – *cantabile* at a slightly slower tempo than that of the allegro's turbulent opening theme:

Ex.35

The orchestra was surprised because nothing is more common nowadays than overdriving a main theme at the end – one only needs the crack of a whip to imagine oneself at a circus. Of course composers often want the final sections of allegro overtures accelerated, and when the main allegro theme is holding the field and celebrating its apotheosis this happens of its own accord: one has but to think of Beethoven's great *Leonora* Overture. Though usually the effect there is completely spoilt by having failed to modify the tempo (which means, among other things, *hold back at the right moment*) in order to meet the demands of the various thematic combinations: the unmodified tempo is already so fast that an extra burst of speed at the end is an impossibility. Unless of course an orchestra is capable, as those Viennese players were, of a breath-taking virtuosity. But since the necessity for it was the result of a mistake their feat left me cold. No true work of art should be subjected to that kind of eccentric exaggeration, even though in a certain broad sense it can bear it.

That the final section of the *Freischütz* Overture can be subjected to such treatment without offending German susceptibilities is easily enough explained. The lyrical theme has throughout been bound hand and foot to the trot of the allegro, like a bonny maiden, captured in battle bound to the tail of her captor's horse – so at the end it is poetic justice that the wicked captor should be unseated and his victim the one who is riding the horse. And so our conductors bring the overture to a rousing conclusion. Year in and year out audiences endure without turning a hair the indescribably odious effect of this utter trivialization (to put it mildly) of a theme expressing the heartfelt jubilation of a pure maidenly heart. Year in and year out people endure this, finding everything in order, talking about the power and vitality of the performances they hear, doing this even though they may have opinions to air about the present state of music (opinions such as those of the veteran Herr Lobe,[8] whose jubilee was recently celebrated by an article denouncing the 'absurdities of a mistaken idealism' and declaring that the 'eternal values of art' were being threatened 'by all kinds of half-baked crazy doctrines and maxims[9]') . . . As I was saying, the result of my exertions in Vienna was that a number of persons heard this poor mutilated overture performed in a very different fashion. People declared they were hearing the overture for the first time and asked me what I had done. Above all the thrilling effect of the final section was incomprehensible: they could hardly believe me when I told them it was due simply to a slower tempo. Actually there *was* another reason, a secret one, which the gentlemen of the orchestra could have divulged. I interpreted the expression-mark on the semi-breve of the fourth bar of the broad splendid opening of the final section[10]:

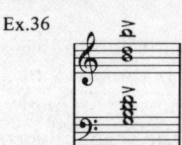

Ex.36

I interpreted that expression-mark, which at first sight appears to be an accent that had got into the score by mistake, as the *diminuendo* Weber must have intended. This enabled me to restrain and inflect the *fortissimo* entry of the *cantabile* theme, and then let it swell out quite naturally at the next *fortissimo*, developing its intrinsic sweetness into a thrilling expression of rapture:

---

[8] Johann Christian Lobe (1797-1881), a flautist and opera composer, had for many years been a notable figure in the world of music letters as editor and author (among other things) of a four-volume treatise on composition.

[9] See Eduard Bernsdorf, *Signale furdie musikalische Welt*, no. 67, 1869 – [Wagner's footnote].

[10] See example on p. 79.

Ex.37

A successful performance such as this is of course by no means to the liking of our Kapellmeisters. Even so, when *Der Freischütz* was given again at Vienna under Herr Dessof he let the orchestra play the overture as they had done under me, saying with a grin: 'This we'll give in the Wagner version' [*Nun, die Ouverture wollen wir also Wagnerisch nehmen*].

Yes – yes – the Wagner version! Believe me, my friends, it would do no harm if a few more things were given in Wagner versions!

All the same, the concession made on that occasion was, after all, complete, whereas the one made in a similar case by my former colleague in Dresden, the late Kapellmeister Reissiger, amounted to only half a concession. When in Dresden I was doing Beethoven's Seventh Symphony, a work he had often conducted, I came across a *piano* marking he had taken upon himself to have inserted in the orchestral parts of the last movement. It had been inserted at the entry – after repeated hammerings of the dominant seventh on A – of the figure marked *forte* which builds up the tremendous coda:

Ex.38

and which sustains its *forte* until at *sempre più forte*:

Ex.39

it leads to the final outburst. Not liking this, Reissiger had converted Beethoven's initial *forte* into a sudden *piano* in order to give himself elbow-room for a *crescendo*. Needless to say, I vigorously crossed the *piano* out and restored the *forte*, thereby violating, I suppose, Herr Lobe's 'eternal values of art' which Reissiger was preserving! At any rate when he did the symphony again after I left Dresden he had second thoughts and came up with the bright idea that the solution was to have the orchestra play the passage *mezzo forte!*

Not long ago at a performance of the *Egmont* Overture in Munich which I attended I had an experience hardly less instructive than the one with the *Freischütz* Overture. That tremendous theme of the introduction:

Ex.40
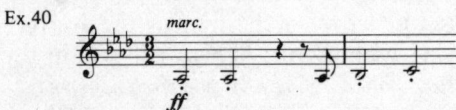

is treated in the Allegro as a second theme; it returns at a faster rhythm in order to be answered by a soothing counter-phrase:

Ex.41

In the typical 'classical' fashion this drastic compression of the theme into a statement of deadly earnestness, fused with a sense of well-being, was thrown like a withered leaf into the uninterrupted storm of the Allegro. At most the effect was that of a snatch of dance-music with the first pair of bars making the advance and the second pair whirled round as in a *Ländler*. It so happened that, during an absence of the celebrated veteran conductor,[11] Bülow was called upon to conduct the overture; taking my advice, Bülow showed how the extraordinary terseness of this passage

---

[11] Franz Lachner (1803-90) Court Kapellmeister at Munich from 1836 to 1865.

can be made tremendously effective if the tempo of the impassioned allegro is held back to give a suggestion, be it never so slight, of that momentary fusion of purposefulness and a sense of well-being implicit in the thematic combination. Since this combination just before the coda becomes immensely significant:

the modification of tempo earlier on cannot fail to lead to a correct understanding of the whole overture. Yet all I heard about that performance was that the intendant of the court theatre had thought something had gone wrong somewhere.

Certainly nobody could have thought *that* of the performance under the aforesaid veteran of Mozart's G minor Symphony, no.40, which I heard at the famous Munich *Odeon* concerts. His treatment of the Andante of this symphony and the success it enjoyed was something I had never thought possible. This movement, with its lovely swaying rhythm, its glowing warmth, which of us in his youth has not sought in some way to make his own? In what way? Why, in many ways! If expression-marks are lacking, the marvellous lilt of the movement takes their place and tells our imagination how it should be performed. Perhaps Mozart left so few expression-marks in order that we should do just this. We could revel in the gentle swell of the quavers:

We could trace the moonlit ascent of the violins, binding it into a single phrase:

The tenderly fluttering demi-semiquaver couplets would be a rustling of angels' wings above our heads:

Ex.45

We would swoon beneath the fateful warning of those repeated C flats (imagining it as a finely moulded *crescendo*):

Ex.46

and from the closing bars draw the blissful sensation of death through love . . . But phantasies such as these were of course completely out of place in the strictly 'classical' performance conducted by that famous veteran. Everything was taken with a deadly seriousness that made one's flesh creep as though one were attending the Last Day of Judgment. The lilting andante became a cast-iron largo; not a hundredth fraction of the time-value of each quaver was spared; like a pigtail made of bronze, stiff and hideous, the movement was beaten out; even the angels' wings became corkscrew curls – one was reminded of the Seven Years War; indeed I imagined myself press-ganged into the Prussian Guard of 1740. And then, just when I was looking around anxiously for an escape, the veteran flipped back the pages of his score in order to repeat the first part of his largo-andante – unthinkable that two dots and a double bar should be allowed to go for nothing. I looked round for help – only to be astonished all over again. Everybody was patiently listening, finding all in perfect order, convinced they were experiencing a pleasure of the purest sort, a veritable Mozartian 'feast for the ear . . .' I bowed my head and held my tongue.

On one occasion, though, I did lose my patience a little. At a rehearsal of my *Tannhäuser* I had quietly let several things pass – even the knightly march of the second act taken at the tempo of a church procession. But then I found that the veteran was so undoubtedly a veteran that he was incapable of converting a 4/4 tempo into a 6/4 one, in other words, of converting two crochets ♩ ♩ into a corresponding triplet ♩♩♩. Such a change is required in Tannhäuser's Narration where instead of a 4/4 tempo:

Ex.47

you have a 6/4 one:

Ex.48
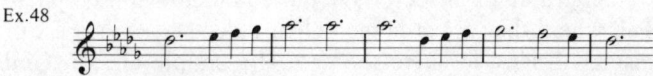

This was very hard on the veteran, for whom the beating of a square 4/4 tempo was an ingrained habit; this type of conductor always handles the 6/4 tempo as though it were a 6/8, that is to say as an Alla Breve two beats in the bar (though in that Andante of the G minor Symphony I did hear each unit of a 6/8 tempo – 1,2,3 – 4,5,6 – given its proper weight). For my Narration:

Ex.49

the conductor, as I have said, made do with an Alla Breve, albeit a half-hearted one, leaving it to the orchestra to make what they could of the crotchets. The result was that my slow 6/4:

Ex.50
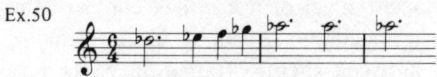

came out at twice the speed as:

Ex.51

This was musically very interesting no doubt, but it meant that my Tannhäuser had to voice the memory of his painful experiences in Rome to the accompaniment of a gay springy waltz-rhythm (which reminds me how once in Wiesbaden I heard Lohengrin's Narration of the Grail delivered *scherzando* as though the subject were Queen Mab). Since my Tannhäuser was no less a person than that glorious singer Ludwig Schnorr[12], eternal values were at stake. I was obliged respectfully to intervene in order to establish the right tempo and this gave rise to a certain amount of unpleasantness.

I have dwelt at length upon the defects of our conductors in the sphere of the concert hall where they are at home. Their defects in the sphere of opera I shall dismiss briefly for here the case is a simple one of 'God forgive them, they know not what they do!' To give an adequate account of the disgraceful things they do I should have to indicate the many valuable things that can be done and this would take me too far afield. I shall reserve this for another occasion and content myself here with only a broad characterization.

In the concert hall conductors as a matter of course take their task with the utmost possible seriousness; in the opera house on the other hand their approach is light-hearted, sceptical, humorous. With a smile they admit that this is not really their element and that they do not profess to understand much about what they are not particularly interested in. Towards the singers their attitude is one of unfailing gallantry: they are only too pleased to supply whatever tempo is asked for, whatever fermata, ritardando or accelerando, whatever transposition, and, last not least, whatever cuts. If once in a while some pedantically inclined conductor demurs, the chances are he will be wrong. For in this sphere, which he does not take seriously, the singer is completely at home; he is the one who knows what can and should be done. Indeed whenever something worthwhile is achieved in the operatic world it is generally due to the instincts of singers – not to mention the good sense of the orchestral players. One has but to look at an orchestral part of, say, *Norma* to see what curious musical freaks an innocent sheet of notes may contain: the mere sight of the key changes -- an aria's adagio section in F sharp major, its allegro section in F major and between them a transition passage in E flat major (for military brass) – gives a horrifying picture of the music to which a respected Kapellmeister cheerfully beats time. Only once in a suburban theatre of Turin (i.e. in Italy) have I ever heard a correct performance of the complete *Barber of Seville*. Our Kapellmeisters are not prepared to take any trouble even over this undemanding score: they do not realise that cultivated minds enjoy a correct performance of no

---

[12] Ludwig Schnorr (1836-1865) was the Tristan of *Tristan und Isolde*'s first production. He died a few weeks afterwards. Wagner's recollections of him are one of the finest of his prose works.

matter how unimportant an opera, simply because it *is* correct. Pleasure – even a sense of aesthetic liberation – can be drawn from the shallowest piece of theatrical hackwork in the most insignificant Paris theatre simply because every detail of the performance is utterly right. Indeed such is the power of the aesthetic principle that even if the performance is only partly successful it still creates an aesthetic effect: we feel we are in the presence of art, even though of a very humble kind. In Germany such effects are created only by the productions of ballet in Vienna and Berlin. For there everything is in the hands of a single person who thoroughly understands his job: the ballet-master. It is he who controls the tempo and expression of the orchestra and this control he exercises on behalf of the *ensemble* with the approval of all – unlike the opera conductor who panders to the individual singer. The result is that suddenly we find the orchestra playing properly – and what a delightful sensation that is everyone will agree who goes to such a ballet after having sat through an opera. In opera the stage manager could achieve a like result; but curiously enough the fiction persists that opera lies in the realm of absolute music. Thus when, as sometimes happens, a performance does come off, thanks to the instincts of a talented cast and the whole company's enthusiastic efforts, at the final curtain it is always the Kapellmeister, whose incompetence has abundantly manifested itself, who is brought forward and acclaimed as the representative of the corporate achievement. Why this should be so he himself must be at a loss to understand; in the circumstances he too might well exclaim 'God forgive them, they know not what they do!'

Since here it is the subject of conducting that I am concerned with I must at this point, in order to avoid involving myself any further with the state of our opera, call a halt and declare the subject closed. To carp at the foibles of our Kapellmeisters is not my affair – I leave it to singers to complain that the beat of one is too rigid or that another is not sufficiently attentive. Dispute is possible when it is a question of purely technical matters such as these. *But from the higher point of view of a genuinely artistic achievement such conducting simply does not enter into consideration.* Since here a word from me is called for – of all living Germans particularly from me – I shall finally permit myself a closer account of my reasons for this outright condemnation.

When I look back upon the performances of my operas I find it hard to decide which of the failings of our conductors I have been discussing is the most relevant. Is it the spirit in which our great music is treated in the concert hall or that in which operas are treated in the theatre? My misfortune, it seems to me, is that in the case of my operas *both* spirits are active. In the introductory orchestral pieces the first of the two is active and the catastrophic effect of the practices described above manifests itself all over again. I need only speak of the tempo which is either senselessly hurried (as Mendelssohn did my *Tannhäuser* Overture at a Leipzig concert – as though to provide a shocking object lesson), or muddled (as my *Lohengrin* Prelude has been in Berlin and nearly everywhere else) or dragged and muddled simultaneously (as recently my *Mastersingers* Overture was in Dresden and other places). Never have I heard those sensitive modifications necessary to an intelligible performance which I regard as no less crucially important than the playing of the right notes.

To give an idea of the utter ruin caused by performances such as these it will suffice to describe the treatment of my *Mastersingers* Overture.

For the main tempo of this movement I gave the marking 'sehr mässig bewegt' [very moderately animated], which is broadly equivalent to the conventional *Allegro maestoso*. In a large-scale work containing passages in which the thematic content is treated episodically no tempo stands in greater need of modification; and when you have contrasting motives treated in different kinds of combination this is a tempo often chosen, since its regular 4/4 beat is very easy to modify. Furthermore it can be read in different ways. Beaten out in emphatically animated crotchets it becomes a genuine lively allegro: this type of allegro, the main tempo of the movement, is at its liveliest in the eight bars of the transition from the C major of the opening march section to E major:

Or it can be read as a 2/4 beat, as in the brisk E flat delivery of the theme in diminution:

Ex.53

Or it can be read as an Alla Breve, implying the older type of comfortable *Tempo Andante* (often employed in Church music), denoted by two slowish beats. This was the tempo I had in mind for the combination of the Prize Song theme with the main March theme eight bars after the return to C major:

Ex.54

For the Prize Song theme when it first enters in diminution in E major I employed a pure 4/4 beat:

Ex.55

When the theme is delivered tenderly this gives it an impassioned urgent quality (something like a whispered declaration of love). In order to preserve the tenderness of the theme – and because the feeling of impassioned urgency is amply conveyed by the livelier figuration – the tempo must be slowed to the utmost limit of a 4/4 beat. It was to achieve this imperceptibly (i.e. without violating the character of the overture's fundamental tempo) that the E major entry was preceded by a bar marked *poco rallentando*. Since the music becomes more and more restless with the entry of the second E major theme, marked *più appassionato*:

it was easy to get back to the original faster tempo. And again later on it was possible to hold back the tempo slightly for the above-mentioned andante Alla Breve, since I would be repeating a retardation already made in the opening march section for the broad *cantabile* development of the initial march theme:

This *cantabile* development had been preceded by a passage dominated by a fanfare theme in massive crotchets:

whose rhythm must have ceased before the *cantabile* development begins, and this it does on the dominant chord in the bar before:

Thereafter the broad swing of the Alla Breve beat had been maintained as the tension increased and the modulations piled up:

Ex.60

I assumed I could leave it to the conductor to manage the beat since when the execution of such passages is left to the instincts of the performer the tempo naturally becomes more fiery. From my own experience I could safely reckon that I had only to mark the point at which the main tempo is re-established, i.e. the E major Prize Song theme entry, which I marked 'Mässig im Hauptzeitmaass' [Moderately in the main tempo]: every musical sensibility would feel the return of the crotchet rhythm in the progression of the harmony. In the same way, at the conclusion of the overture, the more massive 4/4 beat would re-establish itself at the return of the above-quoted fanfare theme, embellished by demi-semiquaver figuration ensuring that the tempo at the end would be the same as at the beginning:

Ex.61

The first time I gave this overture was at a private concert in Leipzig; I conducted it exactly according to the above prescriptions and the orchestra played so excellently that the very small audience, consisting mainly of non-resident friends, demanded an immediate repetition and the orchestra gladly obliged. The event made such an impression that it was decided to introduce the new overture to the regular Leipzig public at one of the *Gewandhaus* concerts. The conductor this time was Herr Kapellmeister Reinecke, who had attended that private performance under me: the effect of his performance with the same orchestra was that at the end the work was hissed. Whether this was intended, whether it was a case of deliberate disfigurement, is a matter I shall not go into, knowing how utterly inept our conductors are. I was told by friends *at what beat* the Herr Kapellmeister took my overture and that said everything.

If such a conductor wishes to demonstrate to his public or to the higher authorities that my *Mastersingers* is an impossible piece then all he has to do is to conduct its overture to the same beat as that which he employs for Beethoven, Mozart and Bach (and which does not do all that much harm to Schumann). Nobody would have any difficulty in dismissing it as a thoroughly disagreeable sort of music. Imagine this poor overture of mine, demanding a tempo so sensitive, so vital, so delicately articulated, laid out on the Procrustean bed of a 'classical' time-beater! 'Here you lie and what is too long I'll chop off and what too short stretch out!' So it would run. And then music is made to drown the victim's cries of agony!

It was in this form – safely embedded – that not only the overture but the whole *Mastersingers* (in so far as it was uncut) was introduced to that same Dresden public which had once heard some lively performances under my baton. Again to put it technically: throughout the whole length of the work the conductor[13] inexorably maintained the stiff four-beats-in-the-bar which he took to be the main tempo and furthermore as a tempo to be taken as broadly as possible. This had the following consequence. I employed the closing pages of the overture, where the two main themes are combined in the ideal andante Alla Breve described above, to bring the whole work to a happy conclusion in the style of an ancient popular refrain: Hans Sachs delivers his pleasantly earnest eulogy of the Mastersingers which eventually becomes a consoling apotheosis of German art to an intensified, extended development of those two themes, here used more or less as an accompaniment. Although the words are serious the effect should be cheering and hopeful: I relied upon those cheerful thematic combinations – whose rhythm, just before the end when the choir enters, becomes broader and more solemn. (For reasons which everyone who knows me will understand I am ignoring the wider dramatic aspects of the work and confining myself to the question of its conducting as though it were a naive 'opera'). Already in the overture the need to modify the initial, march-like processional tempo to an andante Alla Breve had been completely disregarded; likewise the need to modify this processional tempo for Sachs's closing song, which no longer has any direct connection with the march. The wrong 4/4 beat became the norm; the living, breathing portrayer of Hans Sachs was compelled to deliver his concluding speech in the stiffest, most wooden fashion imaginable. Those most closely concerned begged me to spare Dresden this speech: would I please authorize a cut, its effect was so very depressing. I refused point-blank. Shortly afterwards the complaints ceased. Later I discovered why.

---

[13] Julius Rietz (1812-1877), an intimate friend of Mendelssohn, was a distinguished conductor. Schumann's *Genoveva* and *Faust* and Brahms's D minor Piano Concerto were first performed under his baton.

Acting on behalf of the self-willed composer and trusting his own artistic judgment the Herr Kapellmeister had cut the offending speech (for the sake of the work of course).

'Cut! Cut!' – here you have the *ultima ratio* of our Kapellmeisters; thereby they bring their incapacity into perfect harmony within the tasks they find beyond them. They remember the proverb: 'What the eye does not see, the heart does not grieve over' [was ich nicht weiss, macht mich nicht heiss] and the public raises no objection. For my part I am left wondering what attitude I should adopt towards a performance such as this of my *Mastersingers* flawed through and through both at the beginning and at the end, both at the *alpha* and the *omega*. Outwardly it was all very pleasant: the public uncommonly excited, the Kapellmeister recalled, the King returning to his box to join in the applause. And then afterwards the fatal reports of cuts and alterations which, with the memory still fresh in my mind of the completely uncut, completely correct performance at Munich, I found utterly impossible to accept. In this situation – which seems unalterable since only the very few grasp how serious it is – there is one source of consolation, namely, the curious fact that mishandling, however severe, does not destroy the power of the work's effect – that fatal power of effect which at the Leipzig conservatory they warn against so earnestly and which now I myself am forced to rely upon (it is as though I were being punished!). Yet though the writer of these lines could never again bring himself to attend a performance of his work such as that recent one in Dresden of *The Mastersingers* there is nevertheless a comforting lesson to be drawn from the incomprehensible effectiveness of such performances, a comforting lesson enabling us to understand why it is that the great heritage of our classical music is still alive and vital, maltreated though it has been. Such things are indestructible, the lesson runs.

This conviction seems to have become raised by the German genius to a kind of dogma, from which consolation is drawn, and at the same time courage to pursue the task of further creative effort.

III

*On Performing
Beethoven's Ninth Symphony*

ON PERFORMING BEETHOVEN'S NINTH SYMPHONY

A performance I conducted recently of this marvellous work raised a number of doubts in my mind, doubts which, since they concerned the vitally necessary *clarity* of the performance, affected me so deeply that I afterwards studied ways and means of remedying the evil as I saw it. In what follows I offer the result of this study to serious musicians, if not as an incitement to do likewise at least as a stimulus for serious rethinking.

In the first place we must remind ourselves that as regards the instrumentation of his orchestral works Beethoven's position was a singular one in that his view of the orchestra's capacity was exactly the same as that of his predecessors, Haydn and Mozart, though the character of his musical conceptions transcended theirs by far. What one could term the 'plasticity' of Haydn's and Mozart's orchestra – i.e. the distribution and grouping of the instruments – had been the product of a perfect congruity between their conceptions and orchestral technique as hitherto developed. No more perfectly adequate relationship can be imagined than that of a Mozart symphony to the Mozartian orchestra: one cannot but suppose that he and Haydn never had a musical thought which did not at once spontaneously express itself in orchestral terms. The congruity was absolute: the *tutti* with trumpets and drums (only truly effective in the tonic); the quartet of strings; the harmony or solo of the wind, with the inevitable *duo* for French horns – all this was the basis not only of the orchestra but of the scheme of orchestral composition. We must remind ourselves that this was the only orchestra Beethoven knew – only this orchestra, governed by principles that he too took for granted.

Bearing this in mind, we cannot but marvel at how the master with that orchestra succeeded in bringing the utmost clarity of expression to conceptions of a range and variety undreamt of by Haydn and Mozart. In this regard the *Eroica* is just as much a marvel of orchestration as it is of conception. Yet already in that work Beethoven was demanding of orchestras a quality of performance which to this very day is still found wanting, namely, that it should reflect the genius of his orchestral conception. Hence the difficulty of arriving at a judgment of his symphonies ever since the first performance of the *Eroica* and the inability of musicians of an older generation to take a real pleasure in them. Their performance lacked clarity because here clarity was no longer guaranteed, as it was with Haydn and Mozart, by the orchestral organism as such, but made possible only by individual players and a virtuoso conductor with the insight of a genius.

Since the wealth of his conceptions demanded a more manifold and subtly articulated musical material, Beethoven in the nature of the case expected players to provide abrupt changes of dynamics and expression which are the province of the virtuoso. An example of this is the characteristically Beethovenian demand for a *crescendo* which at its climax instead of mounting to a *forte* is suddenly converted into a *piano*. This frequent direction of his is so alien to our players that careful conductors, in order to ensure the correct entry of the *piano* at least, discreetly convert the latter part of the *crescendo* into a cautious *diminuendo*. The cause of the difficulty here is that a single body of instruments is being instructed to do something whose purpose is only made clear when different bodies of instruments alternating with each other are doing it. Composers of the present day who score for a fuller orchestra know this. By availing themselves of their greater opportunities for instrumental distribution they would have been able to realize some of Beethoven's effects without making any eccentric demands for virtuosity.

Beethoven had to presuppose an orchestral virtuosity equivalent to that which he himself had acquired at the piano, a virtuosity in which technical facility enabled the player to articulate with the utmost clarity music otherwise liable to create the impression of an unintelligible chaos. Thus it is through Liszt that his last piano works have become accessible; previously they had been almost completely misunderstood. And if this is not sufficient evidence for the difficulty of performing the later works one has but to consider the last quartets. Here in certain points of technique a single player often has to do duty for a whole body of players, so that a good performance creates the illusion of more players than are actually involved. It is only quite recently that our quartets in Germany appear to have found how to apply their virtuosity to these marvellous works – I recall having once heard them done by a group of excellent virtuosos from the Dresden orchestra, led by Lipinski, and the effect was so unclear that my colleague Reissiger unhesitatingly dismissed them as sheer nonsense.

In my view, clarity here depends upon one thing only: the drastic bringing out of the melody. As I have pointed out elsewhere it is easier for French players than for German to penetrate the secret of performing these works: they were reared in the Italian school which regards melody, song, as the essence of all music. If by this means truly committed musicians have found the right way of performing works of Beethoven hitherto considered incomprehensible, and if we can hope that their methods will become the norm – as in the case of the piano sonatas they have done, thanks to the admirable performances of Bülow – then we can regard Beethoven's compulsion to exploit to the full the technical material of his art – the piano, the string quartet and, last but not least, the orchestra – as a spur to the spiritual development of technique itself – which in turn might lead to a hitherto undreamt of extension of virtuosity. But when, with this principle of bringing out the melody in mind, I revert, as I now must, to Beethoven's orchestra, an apparently insoluble problem has to be faced and reckoned with. Here no virtuosity, be it never so spiritual, can help.

There can be no doubt that Beethoven's deafness had the effect of blunting his aural image of the orchestra, to the extent that he was not clearly conscious of precisely those dynamic instrumental relationships that are of vital importance today when his conceptions call for a fresh treatment of the orchestra. Whereas Haydn and Mozart's formal handling of the orchestra was so certain that they would never have demanded of the delicate woodwind dynamic effects matching those of the strongly manned quintet of strings, Beethoven often disregarded this natural imbalance. Treating his woodwind and strings as two bodies of equal strength he alternated or else combined them, a procedure which works in the enlarged orchestras of our day, but which in Beethoven's orchestra was based on false premises. True, Beethoven was at times able to secure the necessary definition by supporting his woodwind with brass. But he was so lamentably restricted by the structure of the natural horns and trumpets, the only ones then known, that precisely his employment of them to strengthen the woodwind gave rise to passages where a clear delineation of the melody is hopelessly obstructed. One does not have to caution the present-day composer against this evil; thanks to the now widespread employment of the chromatic brass he can easily avoid it – unlike Beethoven who in remote keys either suddenly had to silence his brass or else let them deliver a shrill note here and there, as the structure of the instrument permitted, distracting attention from the melody and harmony.

There is no need to give many examples; it will suffice to indicate how I helped myself out when I could no longer tolerate the impediments to a clear understanding of the composer's intentions. In passages for second horn and trumpet such as the following:

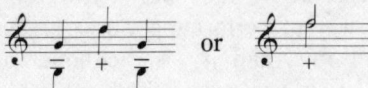

the obvious solution was to have their high note delivered an octave lower:

Ex.64

an easy matter for the chromatic instruments, now the only ones employed. In cases where obtrusive trumpets are suddenly switched off because the

Ex.65

music, without losing any of its loudness, has modulated into a key in which the natural instruments are unable to frame the corresponding interval the solution was not so easy. An example is the *forte* passage in the Andante of the Fifth Symphony (Ex.65):

Ex.65 continued

Here the trumpets and kettle drums, whose splendour throughout two bars has been magnifying everything, are suddenly silenced for nearly another two bars, resumed in the next bar, and then a bar later silenced yet again. Those instruments being what they are, the listener's attention is bound to be drawn to this musically inexplicable procedure and hence distracted from the vital melody of the basses. Until now the only remedy

On Performing Beethoven's Ninth Symphony

I have hit upon is to reduce the loudness of the spasmodically splendid accompaniment, which has the advantage that the melodic line of the basses comes through more clearly. But I eventually decided to take more drastic steps in the case of the highly disturbing effect of the trumpets in the first *forte* passage of the second movement of the A major Symphony (Ex. 66):

Ex. 66 continued

I had the two trumpets – which Beethoven rightly felt should be playing, but was unable to make proper use of – deliver the whole theme in unison with the clarinets. The effect was excellent: no loss was felt but only a gain, and this without any sense of a change or innovation.

I have not yet decided upon an equally drastic remedy for a different shortcoming, albeit of the same type, in the scoring of the great Scherzo of the Ninth Symphony, since I still hope to be able to deal with it by purely dynamic means. I refer to the passage delivered first in C major, later in D major, which one thinks of as the movement's second theme:

Ex.67

Here you have weak woodwind – two flutes, two oboes, two clarinets, two bassoons – delivering a bold high-spirited motive against a figure of four unison octaves maintained *fortissimo* by the full complement of strings:

Ex.68

The support they receive from the brass is of the kind described above: bare 'natural' notes which do more to obscure than clarify. Is there any musician who can declare with a good conscience that he has ever heard that theme clearly delivered? – indeed that he would even be aware of it if he had not read it in the score or played it in a piano arrangement? In the performances one usually hears, not even the most obvious remedy, the damping down of the strings' *fortissimo*, is applied: every time I start rehearsing the Symphony the passage is hammered out with the utmost fury. I myself had always applied that remedy thinking I could obtain a satisfactory result provided the woodwind were doubled. Experience never confirmed this, or only to a very limited extent, because it is not in the character of the woodwind to supply the cutting quality of tone demanded in the context. If I perform the Symphony again I can think of no better way of preventing this extraordinarily energetic dance motive from being obscured – obscured to the point of inaudibility – than to have it played by at least four horns. This could perhaps be done in the following way:

It remains to be seen whether such a reinforcement of the theme would be sufficient to allow the strings to execute their figure *fortissimo* as Beethoven marked it, a matter of vital importance since the figure here is unmistakably that same wildly exuberant one which at the return of the main theme in D minor leads to that marvellous outburst of high spirits which only Beethoven was capable of:

Ex.70

Already I had decided that it would not do to give the woodwind their head by restraining the strings: the whole character of the passage would be lost. What I now finally recommend is to go on reinforcing the woodwind, even if it means using trumpets, until they penetrate the strings' *fortissimo*, however violent. When the passage is recapitulated in D major Beethoven does in fact bring in the trumpets, but again this obscures the woodwind theme, so that I had to damp them down as I did the strings. In deciding such matters the point at issue is whether one is willing to put up with performances in which the composer's intentions are temporarily obscured or prefers to take the steps most likely to do them justice. In this regard audiences at our concert halls and opera houses have become conditioned to resignation of which they are completely unconscious.

At the last performance I gave of the Ninth Symphony I decided to apply a radical remedy for another failure of orchestration due to the cause I have spoken of. I refer to the woodwind's terrifying fanfares in the introduction to the choral movement: the chaotic outbursts of wild despair pour forth with an effect of crying and raving which anyone following the line of the woodwind at the fastest tempo immediately grasps. He will notice too that a striking feature of the woodwind's tumultuous surge of notes is the almost total absence of a rhythmic beat:

Ex.71

If in order to avoid a change of tempo in the ensuing recitative of the basses:

Ex.72

the fanfares are played, as they usually are, at a cautious speed in order to bring out the 3/4 tempo, the effect borders upon the ridiculous. I found however that even the most daring tempo did not free the melodic line of the unison woodwind from the tyranny of a 3/4 beat. The root of the trouble lay once again in the defective trumpet parts, and they could not be dispensed with without disregarding the composer's intentions – those trumpets which all but blot out the woodwind in order to imprint the following rhythm:

Ex.73

♫♫ | ♩ ♪♫♫ | ♩ ♪♫♫ | ♩ ♪♫♫ |

an effect which the master could not possibly have intended: when later on the fanfare is repeated before the baritone's '*O Freunde*', the strings' reinforcement of the woodwind makes this crystal clear (Ex. 74, p. 109).

Once again we see Beethoven prevented by the limited structure of the 'natural' trumpets from realizing his intentions. In desperation – a desperation corresponding very well with the character of this terrifying passage – I took it upon myself to join the trumpets to the woodwind throughout the two opening deliveries of the fanfare in the following manner:

Ex.75

Ex.76

When the fanfare is repeated later they would play as in the first of the above illustrations.

This threw light on the purpose of the whole passage: to create, through the rhythmic chaos of those terrifying fanfares, an overwhelming need for words.

It was more difficult to apply a *restituo in integrum* of the composer's intentions when it was not just a matter of reinforcing or supplementing, but of actually having to tamper with the structure of the score and even with the part-writing in order to rescue a melody from obscurity and misunderstanding.

It is undeniable that Beethoven's increasing inability to hear the sound of an orchestra – and of a limited orchestra at that, which in principle he

Ex.74

[musical score]

did nothing to enlarge – at times led to an almost naive disregard of the relation between his ideas and their realization. Adhering as he did in his symphonies to the traditional rule that violins should never play above:

Ex.77

when his melodic intention took him above that note he timidly adopted the almost childish expedient of jumping to the octave below, thereby interrupting the flow of the melody and indeed spoiling it. I assume that nowadays in the great *fortissimo* recapitulation of the Scherzo's main theme orchestras do not play the passage as Beethoven wrote it in order to avoid the first violin's high B flat:

but as the melody demands:

I assume also that the first flute now fearlessly plays:

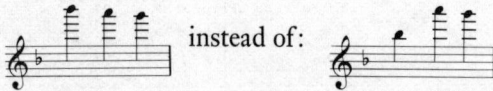

But while in this passage and many other similar ones the remedy is simple, very considerable difficulties demanding more drastic measures arise in phrases for the woodwind where, in order to avoid overstepping a given range – I have in mind especially the flute – we find Beethoven either completely upsetting the flow of the melody or else disrupting it with alien notes. I have in mind especially the flute, the topmost instrument whose entry instantly attracts attention: the listener is bound to be confused if the melody it delivers is mishandled. In the course of time Beethoven appears to have completely disregarded this; for example, we find him giving a theme to the first oboe or clarinet and then for the sake of its higher register bringing in a flute even when it cannot play the whole theme an octave higher and non-thematic notes have to be substituted, distracting attention from the lower instrument. For the present-day composer the bringing out of a melody set in a middle or lower register beneath a superstructure of higher voices is an entirely different affair: he can strengthen the sonority of the lower-lying instruments by choosing a combination of timbres that stand out against the upper ones. Thus in my *Lohengrin* Prelude I was able to bring out and to build up a fully harmonised theme beneath a continuous play of higher instruments and maintain it against every movement of the upper voices.

But this procedure – which Beethoven in his greatness pointed to as he did to every other genuine discovery – has no bearing upon the undeniable obstacles to the understanding of a melody which we must now face. Rather it is a matter of diminishing the effect of a disturbing piece of ornamentation applied, as it were, haphazardly. I cannot recall ever hearing the first eight bars of the Eighth Symphony:

without being disturbed by the non-thematic entries above the clarinet's melody of the oboe in the sixth bar and the flute in the eighth (whereas the involvement of the flutes in the opening four bars, though not strictly thematic, does not obscure the theme, delivered as it is *forte* by the first and second violins). A miscalculation such as this, only affecting the woodwind, is to be found in an important passage in the first movement of the Ninth Symphony. Its effect there is so damaging that in what follows I shall treat it as the principal example of my discussion.

The passage in question is the woodwind's eight bars of *espressivo* just before the close of the first part of the movement:

Ex.83

Who can claim ever to have heard the melodic content of those bars clearly brought out by our orchestras? Liszt with his unique insight was the first to reveal it – I refer to his superb piano arrangement of the symphony. Ignoring the flute's continuation of the oboe's theme, the effect of which is mainly disturbing, he gives the continuation to the oboe, thus preserving Beethoven's notation from any misunderstanding. Liszt's arrangement runs:

Ex.84

To leave the flute out altogether or else treat it merely as a doubling of the oboe at a higher octave would be to go too far: it would be out of keeping with the character of Beethoven's scoring, whose idiosyncratic, yet wholly legitimate, features we must respect. I would therefore leave the flute part essentially as it stands, making sure that it does justice to the melody and recommending the player to moderate his volume and expression out of consideration for the oboe which here must be felt to be taking the lead. I should also recommend that when the flute takes over the melody in the fifth and sixth bars:

Ex.85

the sixth bar should be rewritten as:

Ex.86

thereby preserving the contour of the melody, which considerations of piano technique prevented Liszt from doing in those bars. The only other alteration would be to the oboe part in the second bar. If instead of:

it continued with the melody:

as it does in the fourth bar, then Beethoven's expression-mark <‌> in the two opening bars could be maintained throughout:

Taken at a slightly reduced speed this would impart the requisite decisive expressiveness to this at present grossly neglected passage.

The seventh and eighth bars on the other hand require a single finely executed, clear-cut *crescendo* building up to the poignant accents of the succeeding cadential passage:

In the corresponding passage in the second part of the movement, set in a different key and register, the task of clarifying its melodic content is much more difficult:

Ex.91 continued

Since here the register is higher the flute is necessarily given the preference, and, since its compass above the stave is limited, its part is altered, with the result that the melodic significance of the passage as a whole is obscured. If we compare the flute's melodic line here to the melodic line created by the combination of the oboe, clarinet and flute in the corresponding previous passage:

we cannot but conclude that the musical thought has been seriously disfigured. To reconstitute it would be very daring. In two places one would actually have to alter an interval: the flute's entry in the third bar:

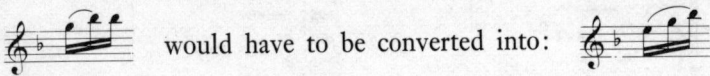

and in its fifth bar: <!-- continued --> . Liszt himself shrank from this: he left the passage as it stands, a melodic monstrosity to anyone experiencing the melodic gap of those totally obscure bars. Repeated suffering has brought me to the decision to have the flutes and oboes play as follows:

In the fourth bar the second flute would have to be silent: on the other hand in the seventh and eighth bars the second oboe would partly reinforce the upper line:

Ex.98

Beethoven's expression-mark would be employed throughout as in the previous passage, except that the different turn of the melody at every second bar would demand a greater emphasis to the ⸺. In the last bar a still more emphatic *molto crescendo* for the flute's desperate leap from G to the high F sharp:

Ex.99

would in my view be in keeping with the composer's expressive intention and set it in its true light.

When we consider how vitally important it is in every musical communication that the melody – which in virtue of the composer's art may often be presented only in its tiniest fragments – should hold us in its grip, and that the correctness of this melodic speech is in every respect equivalent to that of verbal speech, so much so that any departure confuses just as unintelligible speech does – when we consider this we must feel that nothing is worth taking more trouble over than an attempt to clarify a passage or bar or even a mere note in the musical communication of one such as Beethoven, every manifestation of whose elemental genius, however startling, issues from a divine compulsion to reveal the deepest secrets of his world-view to us poor mortals. As one should never let pass a difficult passage of a great philosopher before one has completely grasped it and if one does so reads on with growing inattention, so one should never let pass a single bar of a tone-poem of Beethoven. Unless of course our only concern is to have it performed in strict time by our academic conductors, who will doubtless condemn these proposals of mine as violations of a holy script.

This terrible prospect notwithstanding, I shall offer a few more examples of a well-considered alteration serving to clarify Beethoven's intentions.

The first is that of an expression-mark which serves his intention and yet in performance obscures it. I refer to this gripping passage in the first movement (bars 92-102):

Ex.100

The first two bars of the opening four-bar figure are repeated three times in the ensuing six bars. In bars 96-7 clarinets and bassoons play it *piano*; in bar 98, when the flutes reinforce them, Beethoven puts a *crescendo*; in bar 100 the figure is taken up by the dominating strings and in bar 102 brought to a decisive *fortissimo*. That woodwind entry of bar 98 marked *crescendo* is accompanied by the figure delivered by the strings in contrary

Ex.100 continued

motion and this too is marked *crescendo*. In my experience this *crescendo* for the strings has a detrimental effect: it distracts attention from the woodwind's comparatively weak delivery of the figure and, not only that, makes it difficult to do justice to the *più crescendo* which marks the strings' culminating delivery in bars 100-1. The defect, only slightly noticeable, could easily be remedied by a *poco crescendo* for the strings in bar 98;

Ex.100 continued

but, sad to say, that expression-mark is almost completely unknown to our orchestral players. Perhaps my exhaustive discussion of this passage will have the wholesome effect of drawing their attention to the importance of practising and mastering it.

When the passage recurs in the final section of the movement the closest attention will not help: the unfortunate consequence of Beethoven's failure to carry out his intentions, the dynamic imbalance of the alternating instrumental combinations, cannot be remedied by delicate measures. This applies in the first place to bars 363-4 where the *crescendo* of the first violins and all the other strings creates an effect which the *crescendo* of the clarinets in bars 364-5 cannot possibly continue and carry further:

Three Wagner Essays

Ex.101 continued

Here I had to decide to drop altogether the *crescendo* of bars 363-4 and keep it for the woodwind of bars 365-6 and furthermore have it delivered very energetically since at bar 369 the progression, reinforced by the strings, leads to a full *fortissimo*.

For the same reasons when the passage recurs again in bars 457-62 the first two bars must be played *piano* throughout. In the next two the woodwind must have a stronger and the strings a weaker *crescendo*, which should swell out only in the last two bars before the *fortissimo*.

Since I do not propose to say anything more about Beethoven's expression-marks and what I consider to be the correct way of interpreting them, and having done my best to justify the few modifications I have suggested, it remains to insist that the master's expression-marks should be as much an object of study as his themes since they often provide the clue to a correct understanding of the intention behind them. Also I take this opportunity to point out that when in my essay *On Conducting* I argued for modifications of Beethoven's tempo it was certainly not in order to encourage the witty style adopted – as I have been reliably informed – by a senior Berlin Kapellmeister who when conducting the symphonies made piquant effects by taking certain passages now loudly now softly echo-wise, now more slowly, now faster. Such amusing effects may be in place in a good-humoured performance of *The Daughter of the Regiment* or *Martha*. They are not what I had in mind when I undertook the difficult task of explaining and justifying the correct performance of Beethoven's music.

My endeavours to elucidate Beethoven's intentions in the Ninth Symphony bring me finally to a passage of extreme difficulty in the solo quartet of the choral movement. After long experience I have discovered why, marvellously conceived though it is, in performance it never makes a truly happy effect. I refer to the famous passage in B major just before the close:

Ex.102

Ex. 102 continued

The reason why this passage usually – indeed always – fails is not the high-lying part for soprano at the close, nor the far from easy intonation of the contralto's D natural in the penultimate bar: such difficulties can be perfectly well overcome by a soprano with an appropriately high register and a really musical contralto with a feeling for harmony. The obstacle, only to be got rid of by drastic measures, is the premature figuration of the tenor part which on the one hand blurs the clarity of the total effect and on the other sets the tenor a task defying the laws of respiration, a task impossible to achieve without strain and anxiety. The passage as a whole can be described as an arresting melodic figuration delivered in turn by the soprano, contralto, tenor and bass in free imitation above a sustained six-four chord. Removing the accompanying voices, Beethoven's intention can be expressed thus:

Ex. 103

In the second bar, however, the tenor is doubling the contralto in sixths and thirds. Thereby the sensuous effect of the figure in the next bar is blunted and this robs his part of the importance it ought to have, the more so because the tenor's delivery of the figure reproduces the melodic curve of the soprano's initial delivery. And the effect is further impaired by the difficulty of voicing those two bars of figuration – whereas if there were only one such bar there would be no difficulty at all. After careful consideration I resolved in future to spare the tenor the task of doubling the contralto by substituting only the essential harmonic notes. Thus I would have him sing:

Ex.104

wo dein sanf - - - ter, dein sanf - - - ter Flügel weilt.

I am sure that every tenor will be grateful who has struggled vainly with:

Ex.105

and that he will sing all the more beautifully the melody that is truly his – and making the most of it if he observes the following expression marks:

Ex.106

By way of conclusion I should like merely to mention that I had no difficulty in persuading that fine singer Betz, when with friendly zeal he took the baritone solo in the performance of the Ninth Symphony that I recently conducted, *not* to sing the opening bar of his delivery of the *Freude* melody as it is written:

Ex.107

Freu - de, schö - ner Göt - ter - fun - ken!

but with the preceding bar in mind to sing instead:

Ex.108

Freu - de, schö - ner Göt - ter - fun - ken!

I leave it to our baritones trained in the sterling English oratorio tradition to go on forever venting their '*Freude*' in two strict crotchets.